Twin sis...
Rose's c... ...Lily's breakup have seen to that.
Their careers at Evergreen General Hospital
and their shared house, a cat and each other are
all they need, right?

Except they are in for a twin surprise!

In *A Daddy for Her Babies*

Dr. Lily Carter is good friends with colleague
Dr. Theo Montgomery. And while a chemistry zings
between them, she's not prepared to do anything
about it. She doesn't need another guy who's big
on dating but not on commitment. Except when she
discovers she's pregnant with twins, he's the rock
she never expected...

In *From a Fling to a Family*

Fertility doctor Rose Carter might not want a man,
but she does want a family. And she's determined to
become a mom via IVF. But meeting new ob-gyn
Dr. Lucas Bennett changes all that. Now she's
pregnant with twins—are her babies a result of
the IVF or is their father kind, caring Lucas,
who challenges all her views?

Both titles available now.

Dear Reader,

So we're back in Chicago at Evergreen General for the second story in our "flower girl" twins duet. Lily Carter found her happy-ever-after with the handsome ER chief, leaving her workaholic twin, Rose, committed fully to her work in the fertility department. Writing the story for Rose was a fun one, readers! She is determined to do the whole motherhood thing alone, but in the irresistible gaze of a hot new recruit, will she change her mind? I hope you enjoy the ride!

Becky Wicks

FROM A FLING TO A FAMILY

BECKY WICKS

MEDICAL ROMANCE

If you purchased this book without a cover you should be aware that this book is stolen property. It was reported as "unsold and destroyed" to the publisher, and neither the author nor the publisher has received any payment for this "stripped book."

ISBN-13: 978-1-335-94307-1

From a Fling to a Family

Copyright © 2025 by Becky Wicks

All rights reserved. No part of this book may be used or reproduced in any manner whatsoever without written permission.

Without limiting the author's and publisher's exclusive rights, any unauthorized use of this publication to train generative artificial intelligence (AI) technologies is expressly prohibited.

This is a work of fiction. Names, characters, places and incidents are either the product of the author's imagination or are used fictitiously. Any resemblance to actual persons, living or dead, businesses, companies, events or locales is entirely coincidental.

For questions and comments about the quality of this book, please contact us at CustomerService@Harlequin.com.

TM and ® are trademarks of Harlequin Enterprises ULC.

Harlequin Enterprises ULC
22 Adelaide St. West, 41st Floor
Toronto, Ontario M5H 4E3, Canada
www.Harlequin.com

Printed in U.S.A.

Born in the UK, **Becky Wicks** has suffered interminable wanderlust from an early age. She's lived and worked all over the world, from London to Dubai, Sydney, Bali, New York City and Amsterdam. She's written for the likes of *GQ*, *Hello!*, *Fabulous* and *Time Out*, and has written a host of YA romance, plus three travel memoirs—*Burqalicious*, *Balilicious* and *Latinalicious* (HarperCollins, Australia). Now she blends travel with romance for Harlequin and loves every minute! Find her on Substack: @beckywicks.

Books by Becky Wicks

Harlequin Medical Romance

Falling Again for the Animal Whisperer
Fling with the Children's Heart Doctor
White Christmas with Her Millionaire Doc
A Princess in Naples
The Vet's Escape to Paradise
Highland Fling with Her Best Friend
South African Escape to Heal Her
Finding Forever with the Single Dad
Melting the Surgeon's Heart
A Marriage Healed in Hawaii
Tempted by the Outback Vet

Buenos Aires Docs

Daring to Fall for the Single Dad

Valentine Flings

Nurse's Keralan Temptation

Visit the Author Profile page
at Harlequin.com for more titles.

Praise for Becky Wicks

"A fast paced, beautifully set and heart warming medical romance set in the stunning Galapagos Islands. Interwoven with a conservation theme which is clearly a passion of the author."
—*Harlequin Junkie* on *The Vet's Escape to Paradise*

CHAPTER ONE

It's 8:39 a.m. I lean my elbows on the counter, peering into the back, looking for Margot. She's the owner at Brewed Awakening and she usually has my smoothie waiting by now, but she's nowhere in sight. My first appointment in the fertility department is in twenty minutes. I'm already exhausted thanks to one of the twins—I think it was Amelia—screeching myself and my sister, Lily, to consciousness at 5:00 a.m. The terrible twos are real, double real in our case.

"Sorry, sorry, Rose!" Margot hurries out from the back in her trademark maroon apron, juggling three coffee cups and a bagel in two hands. She sees me and throws an apologetic smile my way before offloading the breakfast items to the people waiting. "How are you?"

"Busy morning," I say needlessly as she reaches for my premade smoothie.

She says I can pay tomorrow, and I thank her, finally making my way back to the door. Chicago's busiest and best café just happens to be on my route to Evergreen General, by way of a small two-street detour and a free short-stay parking space in an old client's driveway right next door. It pays to be one of the city's best known, and thankfully well-liked, endocrinologists.

I swing open the door, just as a tall, strapping black man steps inside. He's looking down at his phone. I'm secretly admiring his height and impeccable bone structure when his elbow unwittingly catches mine, sending both our phones to the floor. I bend down to catch mine, just as he does the same, knocking my drink sideways with his hand. Before I can right myself, the smoothie tips straight from my hand and sends the vivid green liquid splattering all the way down my white shirt. Oh, my…no!

I don't even have any words as I stand, watching the green droplets slowly drip from my clothing onto the gray checked floor.

"Oh, man, I'm so sorry!" The guy quickly picks up his phone and stands back to give me some space. The embarrassment is acute as I try ineffectively to wipe the green smoothie from my front with a handful of napkins someone hands me. The coffee shop has gone oddly silent. My face flushes hot. My pulse drums in my ears. The man looks genuinely horrified. His deep brown eyes have gone wide with shock. "I didn't see you coming," he says awkwardly, running a hand through his cropped black hair.

"Don't worry about it." My voice is tight and clipped as I swipe at the mess, and he winces visibly at my tone, but doesn't back off.

"Let me buy you another one," he insists, holding out his hand for my empty cup.

Bristling at his pitying gaze, I snatch it away from his outstretched hand. "That's not necessary," I tell him sharply. I don't need a man pitying me, whatever the situation. But despite the awkwardness I find myself unable to look away from him as he continues to mop more green juice from the floor with napkins. Underneath the mortification and annoyance simmering in my belly, I'm quite thrown to experience the unexpected flutter of something else. He is undeniably attractive, strapping and handsome, broad and striking, and I haven't seen him around here before. I thought Lily and Theo had set me up with every sexy bachelor in town by now, which must mean only one thing. He is either married, or new in town.

He's brushing away an errant piece of avocado pulp from his own sleeve now. "I insist. Let me buy you another one."

His offer triggers another unexpected flutter in my stomach as I take a moment to really look at him: cropped black hair, smooth ebony skin, a short beard with just the smallest sprinkling of salt-and-pepper gray. No wedding band. His kind brown eyes are full of compassion and a touch of mischief, too, shining behind sleek, black, oval-shaped glasses, which suit him perfectly.

"I'd prefer a dry-cleaning voucher," I say quickly. Laughter bubbles up from the crowd behind us and even *he* smiles, a warm laugh lifting the corners of his dark eyes.

"Right," he says, grinning, seemingly unfazed by my sarcasm. "I would need an address, to know where to send that."

I stare at him, open-mouthed this time. Is he seriously hitting on me after that? Asking me where I live? I should be offended, but instead I'm just confused. I take a step back, glancing down at my stained shirt one more time. This is not how I envisioned starting my day. I mumble that I have to go and quickly deposit the smoothie cup with a disgruntled Margot. I'll pay for it tomorrow anyway, but right now I'm late, and I've nothing else to change into. It's going to be a long day at work, looking like I just had a bust up with a bucket of green paint.

In the consultation room that doubles as my office, I rest my elbows on the desk, stacked neatly with pamphlets and medical journals. Across from me, thirty-nine-year-old Mrs. Emily Hanson is here for her post-surgery ultrasound. She's wringing her hands. "Nathaniel can't be here today," she says.

"You're not alone," I assure her, squeezing her

hand. Emily has experienced two miscarriages, both requiring dilation and curettage to remove the pregnancy tissue. Unfortunately, further testing revealed Asherman's syndrome, in which scar tissue forms inside the uterus. It wasn't an encouraging outcome and she needs our ongoing support.

"How are you feeling now, a month since the hysteroscopy?"

"I don't honestly know," she says, reaching for the box of tissues on my desk. Emily had a hysteroscopy to surgically remove some of the scar tissue. We hoped it would restore the uterine environment.

"Well, let's take a look, shall we?"

I make a little small talk while I perform the ultrasound, ask her about her work, her weekend plans. I smile when she tells me she had sex for the first time since the op on Thursday. My patients often get personal with me, considering my profession. If only they knew my own sorry single status. I'm the biggest walking irony in Chicago—a single thirty-six-year-old fertility doctor in her second round of secret IVF, via a sperm donor at a different facility all the way across town.

As Emily talks about Nathaniel and how amazing he's been through all of this, I can't forget what happened the last time I put my trust in a man. My eight-year marriage went up in flames thanks to his stupid affair. I was so sure David and I wanted the same things. Turned out he wanted his twentysomething surgical technologist—Harriet from Shropshire, England. Maybe it was the accent. Maybe she was just more available and not married to her work. Whatever it was that made his eyes wander, it was pretty clear he didn't want a kid as much as I did, and I'm no spring chicken. Sometimes you just have to be proactive. I always longed for a family, maybe more than Lily did. I want one as much as Emily does, even if I do it alone.

"Well, the good news is that the uterine lining is regrowing properly, and I don't see any new scar tissue forming."

Emily breathes a sigh of relief. "That's good."

"Like I said, it's very good." I smile. Already she looks less nervous. I recommend a second diagnostic hysteroscopy after another menstrual cycle, just to be sure, and tell her we'll then see about our next steps. She puts a hand to my arm by the door, gathering up her purse.

"Thank you, Doctor Carter. You always make me feel better."

"Please, call me Rose," I tell her. "And I know what you're going through. I'm always here."

Empathy is my secret weapon; it disarms fear, builds trust. Lily says I never lost it, even after what David did, and I guess I didn't. My work has never been affected by my ex-husband's betrayal. My work is my life. Although I admit it's been a struggle since the divorce, gathering up all the pieces of me and patching them back together, creating this new version of myself. A single version, who was trying to get pregnant with a loving husband once, just like Mrs. Hanson is now. I still feel gutted when I think how we were trying for a baby by night, while he was having his way with Harriet by day, behind my back.

Only my twin sister, Lily, and her husband, Theo, know I'm trying for a baby alone. I can't sit around waiting for my dreams to come true, or for my prince to ride up on a white horse. Most princes are frogs in disguise, and who needs a man, anyway? Well, okay, I need a man. For sperm. But for everything else, I'll handle it, thanks.

If only the IVF was actually working.

Emily Hanson heads out the door and I follow, slipping into the bustle of the hallway. The sterile antiseptic smell mingles with the low murmurs from several nurses at the station, and I tighten my white coat around me to hide the smudge of green from this morning's little incident. I'm still annoyed I never actually got any of that healthy juice into my system, and I will have to wash it off my shirt tonight instead. But I can still picture that guy. Now, *he* was my idea of a prince: tall, dark, handsome—

"Doctor Carter?" A voice catches my attention on the way to the ladies' room. It's Janet from HR, her clipboard hugged to her chest like a shield. "There's someone you need to meet."

"Sure." Curiosity piques as I adjust my lab coat again. Then I remember the new OB-GYN who's starting with us today. He's moved here from New York, where he was leading some impressive research studies at NYU Langone Fertility Center, on top of his exemplary primary care and surgical responsibilities. They conduct some truly pioneering research in reproductive endocrinology over there. He'll be continuing some of those studies here as he works alongside me.

Oh. My. Goodness. All the breath leaves my lungs for a moment when I realize who's in front of me. It's *him*. Of course it would be him.

My eyebrows shoot up when I spot her, recognizing her immediately. She looks just as surprised, though she covers it quickly. I can't help a bit of a smirk—half amusement, half...well, I'm not quite sure what. I extend my hand, giving hers a firm shake, confident but not over-the-top.

"Pleasure to meet you," I say smoothly, pretending we hadn't already crossed paths this morning.

She plays along. "Likewise." Her gaze lingers a beat longer than usual, taking in my cropped black hair, my face, my eyes. I'm used to that look; people tend to watch me, like I take up a bit too much space. And here, at Evergreen, I feel that sense of command more than I did earlier at Brewed Awakening.

Janet clears her throat, adding, "As you know, Doctor Bennett is our new OB-GYN." There's a bit of pride in her voice, like she's welcoming some kind of heavyweight into the department.

Dr. Rose Carter—I remember her name now, saw it on a few papers while I was doing my own research—flashes a polite smile. "We've all been looking forward to your arrival, Doctor Bennett," she says.

So she knows a bit about me. Well, I did some reading on her, too. A respected career, a few impressive publications in reproductive endocrinology and infertility. She's worked her way up the hard way—that much is clear. No shortcuts. I respect that.

"I've heard a lot about your work here, Doctor Carter," I say, my tone sincere.

Rose nods, but there's a guarded look in her eye. I've seen it before—people who've put in years of work, who guard their space fiercely. I get that. My own journey from New York to Chicago, and now here, wasn't exactly without its costs.

And then there's the way she looks at me, a little too closely, like she's wondering what she'll have to put up with. Like maybe she's had to deal with one too many inflated egos. But that's not me. I'm here to contribute, not compete. And to forget about Mabinty—her tear-stained face when she called around unprompted and saw I really *was* packing my bags to move states. I think that was when she realized it was really over. Maybe that was when we *both* realized we'd reached the end of the road, despite my breaking things off months before. Mom and Dad weren't impressed, having known us as a couple for pretty much our whole lives, but who meets their soul mate when they're a child?

You did, Lucas! said my mom, in tears. *You were perfect together!*

I beg to differ. People grow apart. I said that to Dad, looking for backup. He just held up his hands, went to his office and shut the door, as usual. I can't even count the times I've wanted to saw that goddamn door off its hinges and make him talk to me, his only son. Has he even noticed I've left New York yet?

"I'm looking forward to collaborating with you," I say, keeping it professional, though I notice a flicker of something cross her face. Her cheeks go a bit pink, and for a moment she looks almost vulnerable. I'm not sure if she's embarrassed by our earlier encounter or just wary of me, but she squares her shoulders, regaining her composure quickly and mentioning a few of my research papers and how much she enjoyed them. Respect.

She gestures down the hall. "Shall we, Doctor Bennett?"

"Please, call me Lucas."

"Lucas," she repeats, my name rolling off her tongue with surprising warmth. There's something about the way she says it that I can't quite place, but I like it. I like how intrigued she seems to be by all my research, too. Mabs was never all that interested in my work, in all the years we were together—she had her own ambitions, I suppose, in the tech world. Mabs could never wrap her head around how I could work in a fertility department and still not want kids, either. To her, it seemed hypocritical, impossible to reconcile— even though she knew about my dad. How his indifference toward me taught me that kids only end up standing in the way of your ambitions.

I don't want to think about Mabinty, not here.

I follow Rose down the hall, and I find myself thinking a little too hard about her instead. The green of her eyes, and the green of that smoothie on her shirt that I know she's hiding.

CHAPTER TWO

THE DOOR TO the consultation room swings open, and the assistant presents us forty-one-year-old honey-blond Mrs. Denise Caldwell, dressed in slim-fitting jeans and a designer jacket. "Nice to see you again. Please, take a seat," I say.

"Thank—" Mrs. Caldwell's gratitude is cut short when she clocks the presence of Lucas Bennett, filling the space with his authoritative presence, even from across the room. He was leafing through some of my journals, and admittedly I was half watching him, half texting Lily about this morning's mishap and his surprise reappearance when the door opened.

"Lucas Bennett, meet Mrs. Caldwell," I introduce them briskly, gesture for him to sit in the chair next to me. "He'll be joining us today, and I've brought him up-to-date on your file. I believe he has some insights for you."

"Of course." Mrs. Caldwell nods, her eyes flicking between us with subtle interest. Lucas is so tall his knee knocks mine softly as he settles into the chair.

"Apologies, Doctor Carter," Lucas murmurs with another polite nod, shifting further away in his chair and continuing to explain his credentials. The echo of the contact lingers on my skin, a kinetic spark pulsing through my veins. It's a sensation I definitely did not expect. I stutter on my words when I take over.

"We've, um…we've got your latest hormone panels back," I begin, sliding the paper across the desk. My finger traces the numbers. "Your insulin resistance is still a key player here."

I pause for a moment, letting the information sink in. "These levels—" I point to the fasting insulin and glucose numbers "—are still quite elevated, and that's impacting your ovulation and overall hormonal balance. It's one of the main reasons your cycles have been so irregular."

Lucas leans forward, no doubt seeing the confusion on her face. "When insulin is out of balance, it creates a cascade effect with other hormones, especially androgens—that's what we're seeing here. High insulin can drive up androgen levels, which then disrupt ovulation."

I glance at our patient, making sure she's following. She seems to be. Lucas looks at me to continue and I nod in agreement, picking up from where he left off. "This isn't unusual for patients with polycystic ovary syndrome, which we've discussed before. We'll need to address the insulin resistance head-on to increase the chance of conception."

"But the positive side is that we can absolutely work on this," Lucas chimes in. "We can see about adjusting your current treatment plan."

He looks to me, and I do my best not to sound as surprised as I am as he brings up a new medication used to treat insulin resistance, one that is fresh out of trials and proven to help lower insulin levels, which in turn might improve our patient's ovulation.

Denise looks interested. She's practically bumping heads with Lucas over the table now, looking at her charts. "And look, your testosterone levels have started to decrease a bit from the last check, which shows some progress. We just need to keep moving in this direction."

"We need to be patient, though," I add, looking Denise in the eye, while I can feel Lucas looking at me. He's keen and I like it, but we also have to be realistic. Too many people get their hopes up when it comes to getting pregnant, like me. I can still picture my kindly doctor's face when she tried not to break my heart last week.

I'm really sorry to have to tell you this, Rose, but the latest results show that the IVF cycle wasn't successful this time.

I push the thought from my mind, before I can

dwell on it. It might be successful next time. It can take a while sometimes.

"Hormonal balance doesn't happen overnight. It could take a few months for your insulin and androgens to stabilize and for us to see improvement in your ovulation patterns." I lean back slightly, gauging Denise's reaction. "The goal is to get you ovulating regularly without us needing to rely heavily on medications or injections."

"I know this can feel like a lot," Lucas says, his voice softer now. "But remember, these numbers don't define your chances of becoming a parent."

I realize I'm as hooked on Lucas's words as our patient is. His manner is kind; his input is insightful. I have nothing to complain about here, which unnerves me further. Why? I wasn't ready for this new recruit to be so...what is the word? All I can think is *sexy*.

Mrs. Caldwell seems relieved and pleased as she gathers her belongings, and a tentative smile blooms on her lips as she looks between us. "Thank you, both. It means so much to have such dedicated doctors."

"We're right here with you," I assure her, feeling Lucas's approving gaze on me.

Once the door clicks shut behind her, I turn to face him. Our eyes lock again.

"That went well," he comments, breaking the silence with a smile. He has a nice smile. I noticed that this morning.

"Indeed," I return. Why am I suddenly so flustered in my own space? "Shall we review the next file in the cafeteria? I think you should try the apple pie before it sells out."

"Is that a thing?"

"It's a thing, if you promise not to throw any on me."

He stifles a smile. "Lead the way, Doctor Carter."

"Rose," I correct him, extending the same informality he offered earlier. We're almost at the door when he clears his throat and looks at me sideways from over his glasses.

"About this morning—"

"Don't worry about it. It was an accident," I tell him quickly as the blush hits my cheeks again. "No one has to know."

"It'll be our secret," he replies. Then he leans in slightly, in a way that shifts something around in my system. "But I still owe you a drink."

Somehow, I keep my expression neutral. "What if I'd still prefer a dry-cleaning voucher?"

He grins, and I enjoy his pearly white teeth and sense of humor even more than before. My phone's vibration sends me back to the desk. It's Lily.

"Sorry, I'll keep it quick, just checking if you still have those pearl earrings for the dress fitting this weekend? I can't find them."

I tell her they're in the safe like a bunch of other stuff we don't want the twins to pick up and chew, and Lucas goes back to looking at the books and certifications on the wall.

"Something important?" Lucas asks when I hang up, pulling me back into the present.

"Just sister stuff," I say, smoothing my lab coat. "My twin, actually. She works here, too, up in the NICU."

His eyebrow quirks. "So, there's *two* of you?" The way he says it is nothing short of awed, and his tone sends a lightning bolt up my spine.

"We're fraternal, and she has twins of her own," I explain. I tell him all about Lily and Theo, who also works here in the ER, as we head for the cafeteria. I tell him we also live with a very demanding cat called Jasper, who the twins equally adore and annoy. I probably tell him too much but he looks so interested that I can't seem to stop. Oh, help me. This is the last thing I expected when I woke up to my screaming niece at 5:00 a.m. But I won't say it's the worst surprise I've ever had.

"Stand still for just a second," I say, tugging at the hem of the ivory silk cascading down Lily's slender frame.

"Okay, okay, I'm trying." Lily laughs, her eyes meeting mine in the mirror. "But it's harder than it looks to be a mannequin."

"Trust me, you're a natural." After adjusting the veil, I step back to observe. "This one's beautiful on you," I say. Then I frown. "But it doesn't scream 'Lily' to me."

The dress is a stunning, intricate blend of lace and light, but it's not the one—not yet, I don't think. You know when you just know. My twin nods. "You read my mind," she admits, turning around to admire herself anyway, just as Amelia and Harley shriek in laughter from the pen behind us. The assistant is dangling a lace glove between them, tickling their noses with it, and they love it.

The people at Love Lace, the wedding dress store, have been so nice to let us set it up so we can watch them here, on the nanny's day off. "Do you love the gloves, Amelia?" Lily asks, sticking out her tongue playfully. "Maybe we'll make a doctor of you yet."

"Theo would love that. Next!" I announce, thumbing through the garments on the rack. I can't help the twinge of jealousy at my sister, who has it all. The adoring fiancé, and the adorable twin babies and the wedding of her dreams soon approaching. They've had a long engagement; they wanted to wait till the twins were old enough to know what was going on, and no doubt to ensure they both enjoyed it without tending to newborns all day. Lily and I are alike in every way, except for…well, all of that.

As the next candidate—a softer number with delicate beading—slips over her head, we lapse into comfortable silence. We've been each other's constant, two halves of a whole from the start, and now her wedding feels like another chapter in our collective story. I should be happy for her. I am happy for her.

"Can you believe it?" she murmurs as I zip her up. "This is actually happening. Theo actually chose me."

"He's punching above his weight and he knows it," I tease her. They are perfect together. "Gosh, Lils. Remember how we planned out our dream weddings with those ridiculous scrapbooks?"

"Ugh, yes." She chuckles. "I was going to marry a prince, and you were set on that astronaut."

I laugh, tweaking a loose curl beside her ear, picturing the *prince* who surprised me by showing up in my department last week and threw me off balance for a second time. How has he been there a week already?

"Well, I'm thrilled you found your man, but I don't need one," I say. Weirdly, I'm still thinking of Lucas when I say it and it doesn't quite come out as convincingly as I intended.

"Rose…" She manages to frown at me, despite her reflection glowing with love. I cut her off before she can start.

"Nope. I'm skipping the man part, having a baby on my own. We've discussed this. The next round of IVF will work."

Lily presses her mouth closed. She knows I'm

more disappointed than I can afford to admit by it all, by what David did, by feeling forced to do this pregnancy thing solo. But I've tried the dating apps, more than once. I don't really think it's me; you can't feel someone's energy, or your chemistry, if you meet via a screen, and if it's not there in person when you finally meet, it's just awkward.

Anyway. At least choosing motherhood on my own terms gives me full autonomy over my reproduction and family-building plans. I've built a nice life without a man. Yes, it could be a little more exciting, but still, it's a nice life.

"What about the New Yorker? What's his name? Lucas?"

His name from Lily's mouth sends a jolt to my heart. "What about him?" I say, too quickly. There's a glint of mirth in her eyes when she shakes her head. She reminds me that I spent longer than I normally would earlier last week describing him.

"I don't date colleagues," I tell her simply, and she pulls a face.

"If I didn't date colleagues, I'd never be getting married now," she reminds me. "Don't overlook what's right under your nose!"

I tut at her. "That will hardly be possible. He's going to be under it a lot."

"Then get him under *all* of you." She laughs

and I pretend to thwack her with a very expensive shoe, right before Harley calls out to her.

I watch as she heads for the toddlers, her dress trailing across the floor, and annoyingly I picture Lucas and the way he smiles. I do love his smile. But I really couldn't date a colleague. It would be far too complicated. Besides, I've already decided that I'm going to be a mother. That is going to be my life. I will be a very happy single mother with the support of my friends and family. I can't just be an aunt forever. I want what my sister has, and I want it now.

I'm on the recommended fertility medication at the moment, in the hope that it will stimulate egg production and increase my chances of successful fertilization on the next round. All I can do is be patient, keep up my clean eating, exercise, meditate. Pray for a miracle?

"Hey," Lily says softly, catching my hand. She can always tell when I'm getting too deep into my thoughts. "Whatever happens, you'll always have me."

What would I do without my sister?

CHAPTER THREE

"Needles, hope and hormones," I mutter, scrolling through Emily Hanson's chart. She's due in any second. "Isn't that the unspoken love language of fertility?"

"You make it sound more romantic than it is, Doctor Carter," Lucas says as he leans over my shoulder. His proximity creates a sudden warmth at my back that spreads throughout my chest like it's been doing for the past few weeks. Every time I walk into a room to find him there, my eyes seem to gravitate toward him right before my feet do.

"Let's not scare Emily off. It's her second diagnostic hysteroscopy today," I warn him.

"I'll do my best, Doctor Carter." He catches himself. "Sorry, Rose."

I suppress a shiver when he says my name, not from the cool air-conditioning in the clinic, but from the closeness of this man—this infuriatingly charming new recruit who everyone has kind of fallen for around here.

"So, I've managed to secure a spot for Evergreen at the Dallas conference," he tells me. "I'll be presenting my research on novel treatments for gynecologic cancers. Started it last year at NYU Langone, and…"

"You're continuing it here, I know," I interrupt. "No pressure for me, trying to keep up with all your achievements, right?"

I am only half joking but Lucas grins. "From what I've heard, you can hold your own."

I arch a brow. "I've read everything you've published. Really impressive work."

Lucas feigns shock. "Thanks, but…all of it? Even the dry stuff? And here I thought no one read my papers except my mom."

I fold my arms. "Well, I don't have a lot of free time, so consider that a compliment."

Lucas leans in, smirking. "Consider it received. And if you've read that much, then you know I work better as a team."

"Or a power couple." I catch myself, flushing. "Professionally speaking, of course."

He nods and his smirk lingers, but there's a flicker of something serious in his eyes as I watch him, like he's remembering something. I feel a strange need to fill the silence.

"So, um… New York to Chicago. That's a pretty big move. Why here?"

Lucas shrugs, looking thoughtful. "Could ask

you the same thing. Why do you stay in Chicago when you could go anywhere?"

"Touché. But for me, it's family. My sister, my dad, the twins—they all keep me pretty busy and grounded." I'm kind of telling the truth. My life could be more exciting, I suppose.

Lucas nods. "I get that. Family keeps you... real." He pauses and rubs his jaw. "Sometimes painfully real," he adds, pulling out his phone for a second, then putting it back into his pocket. I'm about to ask what he means, but he's still talking. "Anyway, I like the idea of stirring things up a bit here. Evergreen's got some serious potential, and I want to be part of that."

"Well, you're definitely making waves. In a good way," I say, wondering if my secretly mounting crush is making me too complimentary.

"Glad to hear it. But I wouldn't want to be *that guy* who barges in with all the answers."

I smile. "If you turn into *that guy*, you'll be the first to know." I nudge him playfully, then immediately feel a bit self-conscious and pull back.

Lucas notices and leans just a bit closer, making my heart pound. "I'll hold you to that."

There's a charged pause, and I can't quite shake the feeling that he sees right through my attempt to pretend I'm not enjoying this flirty exchange. But we need to keep things professional here. Thankfully, I'm saved. A knock on the door has me stepping away from him.

"Doctor Carter," Emily greets us with her husband, Nathaniel, this time. Lucas leaves, and soon Emily's legs are in the stirrups—never a comfortable position.

"Emily, I know this isn't easy. I'll walk you through everything, like last time. We're just checking how well your uterus has healed after surgery."

The screen flickers on, displaying a grainy black-and-white image. I'm very pleased, actually. "The scar tissue has reduced significantly, and your uterine cavity is much clearer. The lining looks healthier."

Emily exhales, visibly relieved. I point to a smooth area on the screen. "Your endometrial lining is still a bit thin—five point five millimeters. For successful implantation, we need it closer to seven or eight."

After the scan, she's dressed, and Lucas returns. He discusses the plan for high-dose estrogen and the whole time he speaks, I can literally feel my body reacting to his presence. I can't help comparing him to David, back when we met. The way my pulse would race like this whenever he came near me.

He was deep into his fellowship at Northwestern Memorial Hospital, destined to become one of the country's most sought-after cardiothoracic surgeons. I was on my OB-GYN residency, living a permanent cycle of clinical rotations. It was during one of the surgeries that we met and then our paths kept crossing. I thought it was a sign from the divine whenever I'd catch him in the hallway or the cafeteria. I can still picture the way he'd look at me, peeling off his gloves like he was thinking of much better ways to use his fingers.

We bonded over late-night shifts, shared frustrations with coursework and all the camaraderie that comes with the intensity of medical training, I guess—he had a wicked sense of humor. It was infatuation, lust, my first true love. Everyone noticed the chemistry between us. It was the kind I thought would see us through forever. Everyone saw how it broke me when the truth came out.

Despite what Lily thinks, I'm not about to get too personal with another colleague. I've worked too hard here to risk something like that messing anything up again. Lily and Theo are the exception when it comes to being colleagues and lovers but to be fair, they don't even work in the same department. They make being together, raising the twins and working in the same building seem like a breeze, but they don't have to see each other all day every day; not like me and Lucas.

All that said, it doesn't mean I can't look at and admire, and maybe have a little flirt with, a handsome new colleague, does it?

Lucas is still walking through his treatment plan. I watch as Nathaniel takes one of his wife's hands in his lap and rubs his thumb gently across the back of it, and I recognize the twinge as envy. Ridiculous. My fingers find the silver chain around my neck as I try to will my eyes to stop darting to Lucas's sexy profile. Those lips...so full and delicious-looking.

Ugh, what?

I don't need to be thinking these things about any man. Maybe the next round of IVF will be successful this afternoon. I have to have hope, don't I?

I barely notice the drive to the clinic. My mind is busy on the things I have to do, including a bunch of stuff for Lily's wedding, but my brain goes blank the second my embryologist, Dr. Beaumont, welcomes me into the room.

The walls inside are lined with serene images of nature, a squirrel holding a nut, three galloping horses in a meadow. I'm sure to some people these things are calming. I see straight through them; we have nothing like this at Evergreen. Still, I appreciate what they're trying to do.

"How are you feeling today, Rose?" Dr. Beaumont asks me.

"Just...a little nervous," I admit, forcing a smile. "I really want this to work."

She nods at me empathetically. "That's completely understandable. We want the best outcome, too. Let's take it one step at a time, okay?"

After a brief consultation about the meds I've

been on, I'm prepped for the procedure. As I lie back on the examination table, my heart tries to pound out of my chest. I hate this part. The room is equipped with the most unromantic array of advanced technology, and I can hear the soft hum of machines as well as my own heartbeat as she stands over me.

I suddenly wish I'd accepted Lily's invitation to come with me today instead of being so stubborn, but I didn't want us both leaving Evergreen at the same time and people asking questions.

"So, as you know, today we'll be transferring an embryo created from your eggs and the donor's sperm," Dr. Beaumont explains, reviewing her chart. "We'll be using one of the embryos that survived the thaw from your last cycle. Are you ready?"

I nod, swallowing hard. Of course I know what the procedure entails, but she doesn't have to know that. I was careful not to reveal too much about myself. I guess out of embarrassment more than anything. The thought of anything surviving a *thaw* is even more unromantic than the soundtrack of machinery all around me. Why didn't I just give dating apps another chance?

I have to pull myself together. Remain a sacred vessel. "Yes, I'm ready."

I find myself holding my breath as she proceeds with the transfer. Again, it's entirely unromantic. I could be having sex instead with a hot stranger…but ugh, that would have been even more complicated, and who's to say it would even work? I guess it worked for Lily, getting pregnant from a one-night stand, some guy she met in Miami, but that was Lily. I'm different. I like things to be done, well, my way.

I wince at the slight discomfort.

"Take a deep breath," Dr. Beaumont encourages. "You're doing great."

As the procedure continues, I close my eyes, visualizing this working, picturing myself months from now, carrying a healthy pregnancy. Manifest. That's what Lily would say. Think it, believe it, it will happen.

I'm told to rest for a few minutes once the transfer is complete and I lie still on the bed, feeling a strange blend of vulnerability and empowerment swirl through me. "This could be it," I whisper to myself and the ceiling. I close my eyes again, and Lucas's face flashes into my brain. God help me.

After a while, the doctor returns. "Everything went smoothly, Rose, well done. Now it's time to start the waiting game again. You'll take a pregnancy test in two weeks."

Right. I nod, trying to steady my breath. I appreciate her kindness and empathy, and the fact that she's probably resisting the urge to ask why I'm doing this alone when I could go out and meet a guy. It takes time to meet a guy, though, and more time to trust him enough to try for a baby, and more time to observe him after he's agreed to it, to see if he's changed his mind... No. I don't have that much time. This *will* work.

I'm cornered the moment I step out of the elevator, before I can even slip on my white coat.

"Doctor Carter, glad I caught you. There's been an issue with the Dallas conference next week."

I blink at our receptionist and admin assistant, Maddy, and I know I must look like I'm on another planet, but my mind is still spinning after my appointment across town.

"Sorry, what kind of issue? I'm not involved in the Dallas conference. That's Doctor Bennett and Doctor Lin."

Maddy pulls an apologetic face and follows me into my office. "Doctor Lin has a conflicting arrangement we seem to have overlooked when we were finalizing the schedule. Rose, Doctor Carter, you're the best person to fill in."

She drops the file on my desk with an air of finality and I blink at it. "But my patients, they're expecting me—"

"I've already cleared your calendar. You're all set."

"All set?" The words echo in my head like a ticking bomb before my eyes are drawn back to the door. Lucas is leaning against the door frame now, his dark eyes locking on to mine with an unreadable expression.

"Problem?" he asks, managing to sound both casual and concerned at the same time. I still don't know how he does that.

Maddy tells him what's happened, and he nods like he already knows and tells us Dr. Lin approached him earlier. His elderly father's having heart surgery on the same day. I can hardly blame him for pulling out of the trip.

"Timing's tight," I admit, flipping through the itinerary. "My twin's wedding is coming up and…" I trail off. I realize it must sound like I don't want to go, which isn't ideal, but then, I really don't. I don't particularly enjoy conferences or airport lounges, or soulless hotel rooms and small talk. I'm a creature of comfort. A homebody. I'm also trying to get pregnant.

I'm acutely aware of Lucas's eyes on me as I struggle for an excuse. The thought of the two of us going somewhere, anywhere outside this hospital feels too personal somehow, even if it's for work, but if I say anything I'll look entirely unprofessional. I just have to suck it up; it's only for two nights and three days.

"Let's grab lunch when your schedule allows," he suggests, and I meet his eyes again as my heart does a tiny hop. "To go over the presentation," he continues. "I'll give you some time to look it over obviously, but I'm sure you'll have plenty to add."

"Right, yes. Perhaps. You're the expert."

"Well, you're also an expert," he counters, and he has that look on his face again now, the one that makes me think he sees through me. I try not to let my gaze linger on his broad chest, the pen in his pocket. I'm annoyed at myself. Obviously, he meant a business lunch. What did I think he meant?

He keeps his dark gaze on me as he closes the door softly behind him and steps toward my desk. My heart starts stammering the second we're alone.

"Forgive me if I'm out of line, Rose, but you seem a little uncomfortable with taking this trip. If you really don't want to go I can…"

"It's personal," I tell him. Then I wince. That was worse than lying. "Sorry," I add. "Like I said, wedding planning is a constant nightmare, not that I'm not happy for my sister, of course, and for Theo. It's just a lot."

Oh, Lord, I am making this worse by the second. "I'll make it work around the trip. I'm looking forward to it."

The corners of his mouth twitch, threatening to form a smile. He folds his arms across his chest and levels me with a piercing gaze, like I'm suddenly a specimen under scrutiny.

"All right, then," he says in a calm, measured tone.

"All right, then," I repeat. This is so awkward,

but his smile is contagious. Without saying more than *all right*, we seem to have reached some kind of understanding.

For some reason my heart keeps pounding madly as I exit the room. The thought of heading to Dallas with this man is already putting me on edge.

CHAPTER FOUR

I LEAD ROSE through the crowd to the notice board listing today's events, talks and workshops. "Our presentation's one of the last," I say, glancing at her.

"So many people again." Rose sips from her cup, her gaze skimming the crowd filling up the conference center, and I can't help wondering what's going through her head. She's quiet, keeps to herself, so I barely know anything about her, other than they call her and her twin sister the "flower girls," and Lily has twins herself. Twins everywhere. She went back to her hotel room early yesterday, no doubt to call them, while I discovered a great restaurant with some of the guys. She missed out. And I found myself missing her.

"So, big plans after this?" I ask, testing the waters, hoping to draw her out a little. "Maybe join us for a drink tonight?"

She gives me a half smile. "I'll think about it. Let's see how the presentation goes."

"We're going to kill it," I tell her.

"Okay, Mr. Confidence," she teases, and for a second the storm in her eyes disappears. What is she carrying? Even though I know better than to get too close to a colleague, I'm drawn to her. She's so different from Mabinty, too. It's messing with me a little.

The place feels like a beehive of buzzing medical professionals all trying to make their mark along with new introductions as we head for one of the lecture rooms. We're just squeezing through the third row in search of empty seats when a voice booms out from behind me.

"Doctor Bennett, I had a feeling I'd see you here. Congratulations on the new position!" It's Thomas Marx-Sampson, another ex-colleague from way back in my fellowship days. He extends a hand over the seats and we shake, while I rack my brains as to what he is doing now, and where. I've been to so many of these things, sometimes I lose track.

"This is Doctor Rose Carter," I introduce her, my hand finding its way to the small of her back against her blue blazer—a guiding touch more than anything else, though I don't miss the way she leans into it, only slightly. "We could all learn a lot from this woman."

"An honor, Doctor Carter." There's respect in his eyes and smile and I can tell Rose feels it from me, too. I notice the slight blush across her cheeks before she does that thing she does, where she threads the chain of her silver necklace between her fingers. She's nervous about something.

"Are you nervous?" I ask her as we move through the throng and take our seats with our coffees.

"Maybe," she answers honestly.

"Why? About our presentation later?"

She shrugs, then sighs. "Not that. I'm with a professional, remember, Mr. Confidence?"

"Then what?"

She shakes her head like she doesn't want to bother me with it, but I want to know now. Several people call out to me, or wave my way as they did outside, but I'm continuously aware of her presence right beside me—poised in the blazer and dark blue dress pants, scanning the room with those perceptive green eyes. "We are going to make some real waves with our research later," I remind her, adjusting my tie and nudging her.

She exhales, half laughing. "Let's hope we don't put them to sleep instead."

"No one would want to sleep with you up on a stage."

The words come out well intentioned, but I'm quickly aware of the double entendre and she doesn't miss it, either. "No one would want to sleep with me, huh?"

"That's not what I meant. Oh, wow, I'm making this worse, aren't I?"

"It's okay." Thankfully, Rose is laughing. She asks to see one of my research papers quickly, so I hand her the mobile version on my phone, and our fingers brush. A spark flies up my arm and I do my best to focus on the task at hand, which is to appear like the professional she thinks I am. Or thought I was, until I told her no one would want to sleep with her. Which is not true. Not at all.

"So you seem to be quite the celebrity around here," she says, once I've finished yet another conversation with a guy in the row behind. I note the smile playing at the corners of her lips and try to ignore how the curve of her mouth in my direction sends a thrill to my heartstrings.

"Real star quality, me. That's what my mom says," I reply, flashing my trademark grin, or so Mabs used to call it. Rose rolls her eyes playfully.

"Doesn't it get exhausting? All this…schmoozing?"

"Sometimes," I admit. "But it's part of the job, right?"

"Of course," she says, nodding, understanding flickering in her green gaze. She really does have the most remarkable colored eyes.

"Though, I must confess—" I lean in slightly, dropping my voice to a conspiratorial whisper "—I'm more interested in discussing where we're going to eat after the conference. I know you've never been here before, so I know you've never met real Texan food. You missed out last night."

"Doctor Bennett," she says, her eyes meeting mine, the faux-serious intensity matching my own. "Are you asking me out to dinner when you haven't even bought me my dry-cleaning voucher yet?"

The chatter around us fades and for a moment, it's just the two of us. We're half joking, but we are clearly going to have dinner together tonight.

"Why would I go out alone?" I play on. "Aren't you concerned I might be kidnapped by cowboys?"

She pretends to think long and hard about this and I take her empty coffee cup and place it on the floor under my seat to take away later. Before I can list the steakhouse I have in mind, we're forced into silence. Dr. Lars Henriksen is on the stage. He speaks fluently about how womb-lining receptiveness can be better assessed with the new protocols he's about to trial in Denmark. Rose seems utterly engrossed and scribbles notes right through to the end. I want to know more about this flower girl than I should. Tonight I will be on my best behavior, but I won't let her slip away.

Hours later, I snap the lid shut on the last container of promotional materials. The satisfying click echoes through the now silent auditorium, which will soon be filled with people attending our own lecture. Rose is across the room, double-checking the projector alignment. I can't help but watch her for a second, the way she moves.

"Everything good on your end?" I call out to her.

"Perfect," she responds without looking up. "Presentation is loaded and ready. Oh, hi, Doctor Henriksen."

The Danish doctor has recognized me, but it's Rose who corners him after I've given him an info packet. I wonder why she's particularly interested in him, and it hits me: maybe she thinks he's attractive. He's smart, but he's also not completely awful to look at. I'm comfortable enough in my own skin to appreciate a fellow good-looking man when I see one. I know nothing about Rose's type, but as I watch them talk I spot the tendrils of jealousy creeping over me. Crazy! I'm jealous. I haven't felt jealousy in a long time and it doesn't sit well.

People have started filing in now. Rose slips out to apply some lipstick and I make casual conversation with some of the attendees in the front row. When she reappears, I have to do a double take. From her laid-back look of a blue blazer and dress pants, she's totally transformed herself into a commanding figure in a sleek, formfitting navy blue dress. Every detail exudes confidence and elegance, power and sophistication. Wow.

Her feet are higher than they were earlier, too, but there's no sign of discomfort on her face as she walks in the heels. Instead, there's this newfound confidence in her stride that makes it clear—Rose Carter is here to own the room. As she passes by on the way to the podium, she pats my arm reassuringly. "Showtime," she smiles.

"You look—" I trail off, shrugging farther into my suit jacket, which I pulled on over a crisp clean white shirt earlier. I couldn't help but notice *her* watching *me* for just a few seconds too long.

"How do I look?" she replies, before reaching across and straightening my tie. Her fingers brush against my neck as she adjusts it under my collar, and a red-hot shiver shoots right down my spine. Well, this is just great. This crush is growing faster than I can rein it in.

"Um… You look very nice."

Really, Lucas, is that the best you can do?

Jeez, this woman is getting to me! But she is all business. Her wavy brown hair, that earlier flowed over her shoulders, is now pulled up into a polished updo that draws my eyes to the graceful arch of her neck. A neck I, by now, have spent far too long looking at. Her full lips are highlighted by that bold red lipstick and they're so close now, while she fiddles with my tie. It's all a little too distracting. My brain is about to short-circuit.

Rose's eyes are focused and determined, even as she performs this one small act of attention to detail about my neck, and I catch a whiff of her perfume. It's a subtle mix of floral and spice that reminds me of walking through a souk in Dubai with Mabs… Why am I thinking of Mabs again?

I step back from her, smoothing down the sleeves of my jacket. In the background, the hum of conversation grows louder as more attendees fill out the room.

"You also look the part," she says, appraising me from head to my brown leather-clad toes. "Very suave."

"Thanks to you." I smooth down my tie unnecessarily before following her lead toward the presentation area. The dimming lights signal us to begin, and Rose takes one final look at me before turning to address the room. I can only look on in awe. So this is Rose Carter, the most commanding and charismatic presenter I've ever shared a stage with.

I'm not just impressed—I'm inspired.

Finally, we find ourselves standing alone, side by side. "Well, that went surprisingly well," she says on a sigh.

"You were amazing up there," I reply sincerely.

She shakes her head slightly. "I can't take all the credit. You were pretty impressive yourself."

"But your ideas on how we might continue targeting those *specific* molecular profiles… You have to admit you enjoyed coaching me," I respond with a wink.

She laughs, waves it off. "Oh, please, you didn't

need my ideas. And if anything, you coached me. I shouldn't even be here."

I feel a sense of pride swell inside me at her words. "Let's just agree not to tell Doctor Lin how well we both did," I reply.

We bounced off each other on stage, sharing the spotlight and questions effortlessly. It was like we'd been practicing and collaborating for weeks instead of just a few days, and I can't help thinking Rose and I did a better job at hooking the crowd than Dr. Lin and I would have done, purely because Rose is so magnetic up on stage. There are so many sides and layers to Rose, I can hardly keep up.

"Is it weird that you kind of remind me of my dad?" I say, before I can hold it in. She is going to think I'm crazy.

She raises an eyebrow, smirking. "Remind you of your dad? Is that another one of your compliments, Lucas?"

"No, no, well, yes, it's…it's a good thing," I say. "He had all these sides to him, you know? People loved him. He could impress anyone, even me." My gaze drifts for a second, tangled in a memory.

Rose's voice softens. "He passed away?"

I nod. "Six years ago."

She frowns at me, sympathy all over her face. "Sorry to hear that. Sounds like he must've been a pretty great guy."

"Yeah, he was," I tell her, wondering how on

earth we've reached this point, out of nowhere. "It's just a shame he barely came out of his office when I was around. He could put on a show for everyone else, but he was more of an occasional teacher than a father to me, I suppose."

Her eyes don't leave mine. "Maybe he didn't know how to do both."

I hold her gaze, letting the words sink in. "Maybe."

I stop before I add that for a long time, I thought I could make him see me differently if I just became someone worth noticing. Even graduating med school didn't seem to make him proud, though; he was so self-absorbed.

"You're worth noticing," she murmurs now, her voice gentle. It shifts something monumental inside me and the tension makes me awkward.

"Careful or I'll start thinking you actually like me," I say.

She smiles, holding my gaze again. "Who says I don't?"

"Hey, Lucas!" The familiar baritone cuts into our conversation. I turn to find Ayden Hartlett approaching, his hand risen for what I know will be an exuberant slap on the back.

"Doctor Hartlett," I say, bracing for impact, "good to see you, man."

"Likewise! Been a long time since the Cornell days, huh? Kings of the Upper East Side." Ayden always had this infectious energy about him, like he could make even the dreariest lecture seem like a Broadway show.

"Too long," I agree, rubbing where his friendly gesture landed.

Ayden's gaze drifts past me to Rose, and I introduce them quickly. "Pleasure to meet you," he says, offering Rose a firm handshake.

"Same here," she replies coolly, and I suppress a laugh at the look on her face when he goes in with his standard iron grip.

"I saw your lecture. Impressive stuff. New York's loss is Chicago's gain, right, Doctor Rose?" Ayden remarks. Then he turns back to me. "Speaking of New York, how's Mabinty? Last I heard she was crushing it in the tech world—something about a cutting-edge cybersecurity start-up?"

"Thriving, as usual," I say quickly, though a tightness knots in my chest at the mention of Mabs.

"You guys are still good with the long distance and everything?" he asks.

Rose's eyes flicker to mine momentarily. I can tell she's curious suddenly and I feel completely put on the spot.

"Actually, man, we're not a thing anymore. It's been a while now—"

"Okay, good stuff." Ayden nods before checking his watch. He looks completely distracted. I'm pretty sure only Rose registered what I just said.

"Looks like the next lecture's about to start but will I see you for dinner out at Hank's?"

"I don't know yet." I shrug. I got the invite, of course. Even packed my "uniform" for the event, but I was hoping to hang out with Rose tonight.

Rose tilts her head as he tells me he'll see us later and hurries off, her eyes scanning my face for a moment too long. "Hank?"

"Doctor Henry Jackson Merrick," I explain, pointing at him over the crowd; he's pretty hard to miss. "Most people just call him Hank or Tex. He's another friend of ours from way back, an ex–trauma surgeon. He quit his medical practice to build a quiet life out here, on his family ranch."

"Sounds a lot less traumatic."

"The dinner is kind of a regular event. He just aligned it with the end of the conference this time. So, you wanna go?"

"I'll pass, thanks. Got some reading to catch up on."

Disappointment unsettles me but I do my best to keep it off my face. "Are you sure? Could be fun. It's always fun. You don't want to miss this food, either."

"Then why am I only just hearing about this? I've nothing to wear." She shakes her head, a strand of wavy hair falling from her updo into her view while I scratch my neck. Busted. I didn't tell her earlier because from the way she retreated from the crowds last night, I had a feeling she wouldn't want to go, and I wanted to hang with her *somewhere*. But I'm not going to say that.

"We can go back to the dinner plan, just the two of us?" I try.

"I'm pretty tired," she says. "It's been a long day...my feet are killing me."

"That'll be your choice of shoe," I remind her, and she winces.

"No pain, no gain, Lucas."

We walk to the elevators. We've seen all the lectures we were planning for today and I admit I'm tired, too. Nothing a nap won't fix for me, but Rose seems to have made her choice. I respect that, even if I don't like it. Maybe it's even for the best. If anyone else plans on bringing up Mabs, I'd rather she didn't hear it. I can do without that following me to work, and there's something fresh and new about Rose that I don't want tainted by my past, even if she's subtly telling me that she doesn't mix business with pleasure whatsoever, anyway. If only my heart would accept defeat as fast as my brain.

CHAPTER FIVE

THE TAXI PULLS to a stop on the crunch gravel. I take in the lights from the porch that's wrapped around the homely-looking, tree-hugged farmhouse. I can't believe I'm here, on an actual ranch in Texas. I can't believe Lily persuaded me. I also can't believe Lucas is actually wearing cowboy boots.

"I'm kind of glad I didn't get this memo," I say as he opens the door for me. I gesture to the light brown leather boots he's tucked faded jeans into. His plaid shirt stretches like a tight tease over his sculpted, broad frame, and he flashes me that grin that almost knocks me off my feet whenever I see it, shutting the door behind me and placing a tawny-brown cowboy hat on his head.

"Oh, you'll get it soon. Trust me, ma'am," he says with a nod of his hat that makes me laugh despite myself. Then his hand finds the small of my back again, like it did earlier in the lecture room. The contact sends the same bolt of red-hot adrenaline up my spine as he guides me past the paddocks toward the path. What am I doing here?

I had every intention of lying low in my hotel room again and catching up on my reading, and praying that a miracle pregnancy might occur inside me if I just keep still and quiet. Besides, Lucas unnerves me for reasons I can't afford to contemplate any further. But when Lily called, her reaction was not what I'd expected.

Are you crazy? You would rather sit in your hotel room alone than have a fun night out with your sexy colleague under the stars? You never have fun, Rose. Go have some, I beg of you.

She's such a romantic. I had to remind her that *my sexy colleague* is exactly that, a colleague, and therefore not someone I should be contemplating sitting under any stars with.

I told her, *No, Lils, remember what happened with David? Getting personal with any more sexy colleagues is not on my agenda.*

Then I had to finally admit that, yes, okay, I am madly attracted to him. I just wish I weren't, *especially* considering I am—hopefully—about to become a single mom!

"Lucas, my man, so good of you to come!" Hank finds us as we step onto the porch. His booming voice echoes out over the guests who are already here, mingling in the muggy evening air. His arm shoots out to wrap Lucas in a bone-crushing embrace. Hilariously, he's also clad in the quintessential rancher's attire and now that I'm looking around, I notice that every guy here has dressed the part. In fact, if someone typed in "show me a group of ranchers," I'm pretty sure Hank and Lucas, and everyone else on this porch, would appear in the search results.

"You must be Rose!" he booms as his eyes land on me. Then he envelops me in an unexpected hug. It's like being embraced by an affectionate grizzly. "We've got some good old Texas barbecue waiting for y'all later, but in the meantime, can I offer you some refreshments?"

He leads us across what suddenly feels like a cowboy costume party, toward a rustic wooden table laden with bottles of wine and platters of home-cooked food. Through the window I can see into the cozy kitchen, where more people are standing around mingling and laughing. I wish Lily were here. She's the social one, not me. Before her ex, Grayson, killed all the joy left in her soul, which was long before she met the amazing Theo—who has since instilled it all back in again, thank goodness—she had no qualms about heading out places on her own and just seeing who crossed her path.

Lily lives by the mantra that a stranger is a friend you haven't met yet, whereas for me, even standing in an elevator with more than one person fills me with dread. Somehow, I can switch it on when I'm at work. I show them the side they need to see. It's called playing the game...like Lucas with his schmoozing. Although secretly, I think he enjoys it. There's more to him than I first thought. When he told me about his dad passing away earlier I felt his pain. It's obvious there is something unresolved there, too.

"Hank, you always were the host with the most," Lucas is saying now, accepting a cold beer from an ice bucket. No drinking for me. I have to stay a healthy vessel. I opt for a soda water and steal another glance at Lucas, who seems completely at ease here beneath the wide Texas sky. As for me, I feel a little underdressed now in simple jeans, a loose white shirt over a tank, and feminine sandals. After today in heels my feet aren't yet back to normal.

Lucas catches me looking around. His deep brown eyes hold mine and he shrugs lightly, a half smile pulling at one corner of his lips. "First time at anything cowboy themed?" he asks.

"How did you guess? I didn't even bring a hat."

"Well, we can fix that." He puts his beer down, removes his hat and deftly places it on my head. My breath catches as he steps up close and adjusts it, and I feel another flutter somewhere around my heart that zips me right back to when I fixed his tie earlier. I don't know what possessed me to do that, other than a need to be close to him, to fill my lungs with his cologne and have him look every inch like my partner. My professional partner, of course.

I step away, lowering my gaze. I should have stayed in the hotel room. But I can't lie; I'm intrigued to know more about him now, especially after learning he has a recent ex. Lucas looked more than a little disgruntled to hear that name brought up. What was it? Something exotic. Mabinty?

I knew there was another reason he left New York, besides the job opportunity at Evergreen. Maybe it was a really bad breakup. So bad that he felt like he couldn't stay. Maybe everything in the city reminded him of her. Okay, I'm getting carried away, letting my imagination create the story, but from the look on his face I could tell whatever happened with Mabinty hit him hard. Maybe as hard as the breakup with David hit me. I wonder what happened.

As if I've conjured him with my mind, Ayden nudges his way through the throng and slaps Lucas's shoulder dressed, as predicted, in a flannel shirt, jeans and boots complete with buckles. I'm accosted by one of the women, but as I sip my soda water and make polite responses, I can't help but overhear some of their conversation.

I'm pretty sure I hear the name Mabinty again, but I can't make out the context this time. I can only keep sneaking glances at Lucas's face. Uncomfortable doesn't cover the look on it. Why am I itching to nudge back in there and listen for real? It's absolutely none of my business. I have no reason to want to know anything about Lucas's personal life, and I need to remember that. I'm choosing motherhood over men. *Especially* men who are colleagues.

By the time we're told to gather around the huge dining table on the porch behind the house, I'm feeling better about being here. It's actually nice to talk to people I've never met. How did I forget what new perspectives that can bring?
"I knew there'd be hay bales," Lucas says with a smirk when we spot them scattered around the dance floor. A stage just off the porch seems to be featuring a rotation of wannabe musicians from guitarists to saxophonists and someone with a harmonica who only seems to know one song. Next to it, a bucking bronco sits in the corner on a padded platform, daring anyone to try their luck. The air is thick with the smell of barbecue, and I sneak in a message to Lily.

Is it weird that I kind of want a Texan ranch of my own now?

She replies:

I told you you'd have fun. You should trust me more often, sis. How is Lucas looking tonight?

You wouldn't believe me if I told you.

After I reply I shove my phone away as Lucas leans in.

"So, Rose," he says up close to my ear, giving me another whiff of his cologne and sending a tingle through me. "I'm guessing you're not a fan of country music?" He lifts his hat off my head and puts it back on his, then gestures toward the stage where a guy is setting up a guitar and a mic.

"I wouldn't say I'm a die-hard fan, but I wouldn't turn it off, either." I smile, refusing the bottle as he goes to add a splash to the waiting wineglass by my checkered place mat. Despite my best efforts to maintain composure, I can't help but steal glances at his biceps straining in his rolled-up shirtsleeves as he tops up someone else's glass. I notice he himself has switched to iced tea. He catches me looking and I pull my eyes away quickly.

The sun dips lower as we tuck in to the feast. It's nothing short of mouthwatering: smoked brisket, fall-off-the-bone ribs and spicy sausage links sitting alongside the bowls of creamy coleslaw, baked beans and buttery cornbread. Juicy steaks sizzling on the grill, sides of creamy mashed potatoes and a medley of freshly picked vegetables smell so good. I promised to eat healthily, give my potential baby what it needs, but one night off won't hurt, will it? I'll just add a few more vegetables than meat chunks.

As we dig in, conversation flows easily among the group, though I'm acutely aware of Lucas's presence next to me. His laughter is rich and genuine, and it's hard not to be drawn in. I wonder what Mabinty looked like. I wonder how long they were together.

"Rose, try the cobbler," someone suggests, snapping me out of my thoughts.

"Thanks, I will," I reply, accepting the bowl as it's thrust at me. The sweet, tangy taste of peaches melts with the crumbly, buttery topping and I wish I'd bought some plastic containers for leftovers.

"My sister would love this. She's such a foodie," I tell Lucas, spearing a slice of peach. "She goes to every new steakhouse the moment it opens with Theo, and they always share every dessert wherever they go. They're obsessed."

He smiles, carving into his steak with precision. "And what about you?"

"What about me?" I say.

"What are you obsessed with?"

The way he says it makes me swallow too hard, and for a second it's a struggle not to choke on my peaches. "I guess I'm obsessed with details," I tell him. Why can I command an entire auditorium of people to hang on my every professional word, yet I can't hold a conversation with an attractive man without turning into a hot mess?

"Details?"

"I like to know things are in order," I tell him. God, I sound so boring. He must think I'm so dull. "I guess it's some form of undiagnosed OCD, or maybe I'm just a control freak," I continue, while simultaneously willing myself to shut up and stop talking. I'm not painting an attractive picture of myself here. But he's still smiling.

"What do you do when you're not working? Do you have any bizarre hobbies? Do you crochet while using a Hula-Hoop? Do you have a secret passion for taxidermy, or maybe you're a silent pro in the competitive dog grooming world on weekends?" His brown eyes sparkle with amusement as he swirls the ice cubes around in his glass.

I laugh. "Well, I wouldn't call my hobbies bizarre per se. I do like to garden. Our house has a small lawn out back that I've turned into a sort of urban oasis."

Again, yawn.

"An oasis in Chicago? That's impressive," he remarks. He sounds genuine.

"I wouldn't go that far. I have a couple of rosebushes and some herbs. It's not much, but it's enough to keep me busy and clear my head from all this baby stuff."

I pause. I didn't mean to say that.

"You mean with Lily's twins?" he asks, frowning. "Aren't they toddlers?"

"Yes…yes…toddlers. I just can't help still thinking of them as babies, you know?"

He nods again over his drink. Yikes. I hope I covered that up convincingly. It's a little too soon to tell him I'm trying for a baby on my own, so far with zero luck. It really is the worst situation for a control freak.

"Gardening can be a kind of therapy," Lucas responds thoughtfully after a pause, stabbing at a peach slice absently with his fork. He's watching a man climb onto the bucking bronco, and a few others follow him, crowding around. "My ex used to grow these tiny little tomatoes on our balcony. They never got sweet enough for us to eat. The birds didn't mind them, though."

"Mabinty?" I say. The name slips out before I can stop myself. Lucas shifts in his seat. A muscle twitches along his jawline as he takes another long sip of iced tea, the cubes clinking against the glass in the quiet that descends. Even the laughter around us sounds distant now.

"Yes," he says, setting down his fork with finality. A tension simmers under the surface, and I regret prying.

"It's just…your friend Ayden," I explain. "Sorry, I didn't mean to—" I start, but Lucas interrupts with a dismissive wave.

"It's okay. Ayden knows her, too, obviously."

The silence stretches out a moment longer and verges on uncomfortable. I have a feeling I should keep my mouth shut, but now I just want to know. "So, is she the real reason you moved to Chicago? I know bad breakups can make us switch gears pretty fast. I went through one myself, not long ago. Well, actually, I guess it was quite long ago now but you never really get over the big ones, do you?"

His eyes flicker with something unspoken, and for a second, something tender as he studies my eyes then looks away. "Let's not talk about this right now," he says coolly. "I was having a nice time."

Oh, no.

I maintain my composure as usual, but the heat creeps out from my shirt and up my cheeks as I sit back in my chair. I crossed a line. As for my babbling on about myself, too, why did I say all that?

Cries of laughter echo out from around the bucking bronco. A few people move to the dance floor and start kicking up their boots, and the moonlight shimmers across the pond behind it. I wish I could swim in it. It's the kind of pond that looks like it would be perfect for a moonlit swim; maybe I could sneak off there and hide in it for the rest of the night.

More food is brought to the table on giant heaped plates. This never-ending spread is a feast for the senses, but suddenly, I'm not even remotely hungry. This could be the perfect time to use the bathroom.

"I should probably—"

"I tried my hand at guitar once," Lucas says, halting me in action just as I'm about to excuse myself from the awkward silence. The guitarist on stage has started to play a country tune now. "My fingers didn't agree with it, though, so I switched to piano instead."

"Piano?" I raise an eyebrow in surprise. "That's something I wouldn't have guessed."

"I'm full of surprises," he murmurs. "I'm sure I also don't look like the kind of person who'd creep through a window of an abandoned building just to check the mail."

I can't suppress a smile. I'm so glad that the awkward moment has passed. "What are you even talking about?"

"There's something beautiful about places forgotten by time, don't you think? Forgotten treasures, rusty and torn-up clues about the people who used to live in them. You never know what you're going to find."

I look at Lucas for a moment, picturing him in full explorer's attire, rummaging around dusty old attics and breaking into locked basements, before shaking my head. "Well, well," I say, running a hand through my loose hair. "Doctor Bennett, you *are* full of surprises."

He nods. "The thing is it's pretty hard to find

anything unexplored or abandoned in a big city. You usually have to get away into the suburbs or outskirts. The Midwest is the best, so I've heard. Maybe I'll find some fun places outside Chicago. You'd be amazed how many factories, schools, even whole neighborhoods got abandoned when places like Detroit and Toledo went under. There's this group I'm in—we travel around the country checking them out. It's called urbex. Urban exploration. Total adrenaline rush."

"I'm hooked already," I say, leaning closer. "So tell me... What's been your favorite exploration so far?"

Somehow, my earlier slipup is forgotten. My legs have swiveled on their own to face his, and his have done the same to mine.

"Well, closer to my old hood in New York, there was this abandoned mayonnaise factory on the outskirts of Brooklyn," he starts, his brown eyes lighting up with excitement. "It was massive. Completely dilapidated. Mesh metal walkways, dripping pipes... We had to climb through broken windows and crawl under rusted machines to get inside."

I listen intently as he describes the eerie atmosphere of the place and how they found a bunch of old machinery and equipment still inside. "But the best part was this old office, completely untouched," he continues, his face breaking into a grin under his cowboy hat. "There were papers scattered everywhere, like whoever worked there just got up and left one day and never went back. We found some jars of mayo, too, but we didn't dare open those."

"That's crazy," I say in amazement.

"We found some old documents and letters dating back to the nineteen-fifties. A warrant for evacuation. Reminders of unpaid rent."

"Wow," I say. "You have the best way of bringing these places to life, like I can actually see them."

His eyebrows lift. "You *can* actually see them, if you like?"

"Maybe," I say, swirling my drink. "Not that I'm into urbex or anything, but… I don't know. Sometimes I feel a bit like I've let other things in my life stay on the sidelines, you know?"

He leans in a bit, genuinely listening. "Yeah? So what's holding you back?"

I laugh lightly. "It's probably just me. I've shut myself off more than I thought, especially since the divorce. Most people don't see it—David knocked my confidence, you know? But you seem to have this…freedom."

He watches me for a moment, processing the fact that I'm divorced. I think he's going to ask me about it, like I asked about Mabinty, but instead he gets a mischievous spark in his eyes. "Maybe you just need someone to show you the ropes, as an urbex newbie."

I raise an eyebrow. "You volunteering?"

He grins. "Ever heard of any good abandoned spots around Chicago?"

I think for a second, then shake my head. "No, sorry."

His smile widens. "I'll find somewhere. Then maybe we'll go on an adventure together. See if there's a new urban explorer at this table, hmm?"

I laugh, feeling a flicker of excitement. "All right, if you promise not to get us arrested."

"Deal," he says, eyes twinkling. "Just don't blame me if you get hooked."

My heart jumps at the idea of being somewhere exciting with him. "I won't get hooked, don't worry. I'm too sensible."

"Ah, yes, there she is. The control freak." He winks, and I shove his shoulder playfully, making him laugh.

"I'm teasing you! I'm a control freak, too, goes back to my childhood. Anyone will tell you."

"Oh, yes? Why?"

His grin fades for a moment, and he shrugs. "Aren't all kids control freaks in a way?"

I look at him maybe longer than I should, eyebrows quirked, but he doesn't elaborate. I ask if he has any siblings, because I realize I don't even know.

He tells me no. "It was just me, Mom and Dad. They were both only children, too. So I had no siblings, no aunts, no uncles, no cousins."

"Then you did get to control everything," I say with a smile.

"Nah, my father did," he replies quickly, before looking away and swigging his drink.

"Oh?" He's got that darkness on his face again, the same one he had before when he talked about his dad, and it sparks a need to know more, even though I also know it's probably not the time to go into our personal histories; not that deeply, anyway.

I need to loosen up a little myself. Everything has been so intense lately, what with all the fertility stuff, and Lily's wedding planning, not to mention work. But it doesn't have to be my entire life. Maybe I *could* be the kind of person who climbs through windows with a flashlight and rummages through cobwebby corners for trinkets. At least I'd contemplate it with someone like Lucas.

What is going on with my brain? That would be a terrible idea! For a million reasons!

Before we know it, it's almost midnight. We have barely spoken to anyone else at the table and Lucas says we should go watch the guys take turns on the bucking bronco. His light, steadying touch on my lower back again makes my breath catch. It's been ages since someone has escorted me anywhere with such casual intimacy. The sensation is foreign yet comforting, and it ignites another flutter in my stomach, the kind I thought

I'd never feel again after a string of terrible dates over the past couple years.

"Watch your step," he says as we approach the rodeo arena. His grip firms to guide me over the uneven ground and I can't help thinking he likes touching me as much as I like him doing it. The butterflies are mounting, causing a riot.

The cheers crescendo as another guy, who's all swagger and denim, mounts the fake bull. I think someone's put it on the highest setting because it bucks wildly in a manic dance of man versus mechanical beast, and for a moment I'm swept up in the collective thrill witnessing this bizarre spectacle. What on earth would possess someone to want to do this? Maybe Lucas is planning on it, I think in both horror and excitement. He'd look hot up there.

Then, a snap of reins and the cowboy is airborne before he's crashing down hard beyond the protective surface of the padded surroundings. The crowd's elation morphs into gasps of horror.

"Lucas!"

I don't think. I just react.

CHAPTER SIX

THE COWBOY IS lying crumpled with his leg at an unnatural angle. The pain is etched across his face as he tries to clutch his knee to his chest and fails. "I can't feel my leg too good," he grits out, panic sharpening his Texan drawl.

"Everyone, give us space!" Lucas barks to the onlookers. They obey, parting like the Red Sea. Most of them are medical professionals here and one has gone to fetch a bag already. A couple of the others are on their phones. Lucas drops to one knee beside the man right next to me.

"Keep still," he commands, stabilizing his neck, while my hands palpate for fractures.

"Sir, can you tell me your name?" I ask, needing him lucid, needing to gauge his awareness.

"Ty," he chokes out. The sweat is beading his brow. His hat is lying facedown in the dirt several feet away and his right leg is twisted unnaturally. He's clearly in agony. Hank appears through the crowd, unzipping his trauma kit, but like many of the guys surrounding us he's slightly unsteady on his feet thanks to downing a few too many cold beers, so Lucas takes over and begins preparing the necessary equipment.

"Open fracture. Lower leg—looks like the tib-fib," I tell him.

"Yeah, that's a nasty one," Lucas agrees, already pulling out gloves and gauze pads. "Bleeding's not too bad, Ty, but we've got to splint you up pretty fast, okay?"

Ty is a medic himself from what I'm hearing in not so quiet conversation snippets all around me, and he's doing his best to cooperate through the searing pain. His eyes close suddenly and he drags a deep breath through his nose, and then another through his teeth before trying to move again.

"Hey there, can you hear me?" I keep my voice calm but firm. "I need you to stay as still as possible, all right?"

The man grimaces, beads of sweat dotting his forehead. "I'm trying, Doc…"

"Doctor Carter. Rose."

"Rose. My leg… It hurts so bad."

"I know, I know. We're going to fix you up," I reassure him while taking his pulse, checking his level of consciousness. He seems a little dopey on top of his injury but then, everyone's had a few drinks tonight. Hank leans toward the radio he has somehow produced.

"We've got a male, early forties, open fracture

of the right tib-fib. Prepping him for transport. Is someone coming? What's the ETA?"

"I'm going to immobilize your leg first," Lucas says. He is already wrapping a tourniquet above the break to control any potential blood loss, and a woman is pushing through the crowd to reach them. Ty's partner? "Ready for the splint?" Lucas says, while the woman shrieks at the sight of his leg. His wife is apparently not a doctor. She's just come back from the bathroom to find her husband on the ground.

I hold Ty's leg carefully to keep it steady while Lucas's hands move deftly to place the inflatable splint around it. We all know his leg needs to stay absolutely still before they can transport him. Ty knows, too, but when you're in this much pain it's hard to think straight. Hank leans over him, his broad frame blocking the light momentarily.

"Ty. You're doing great. Okay, man? Just breathe."

Lucas meets my eyes and I bite back a smile. Hank is the trauma doctor here, but he's too drunk. Not that this was anyone's fault; accidents happen. Ty grits his teeth, but nods. "I can't feel my toes now."

I sense my expression tighten for a moment as I check his toes for any signs of circulation. "Pulses are still weak, but present," I confirm to Lucas.

"Got it. Let's get him on the backboard before the pain gets worse," he replies, grabbing the board from the three or four men who are hovering with it on the periphery, awaiting our instructions. I let them help Lucas with this one. "On three?"

Ty still doesn't quite appear to know what's going on, exactly. All he knows now is pain. "Ty, we're going to lift you now. Try to keep still. It'll hurt, but it's important."

"I know," he breathes, bracing himself.

The guys move together smoothly, lifting Ty onto the backboard, careful to keep his broken leg in the proper position.

"Ambulance is en route," Hank informs us.

I adjust the oxygen mask over Ty's face. "You're doing great. Ambulance is a few minutes out, and they'll get you some strong pain relief once you're in the truck."

Within moments, the wail of sirens cuts through the air, and the ambulance pulls up. The team moves swiftly, transferring Ty into the back of the vehicle. His wife hops in with him, and Hank shuts the doors behind them.

As the ambulance speeds off, I'm filled with both relief and adrenaline, and beside me Lucas is wiping the sweat from his brow and putting his hat back on.

"Just another day at the rodeo," he mutters, and I can't help a snort of laughter escaping my mouth. I'm just so tired now; that was mentally exhausting.

"Everyone all right?" Hank's voice cuts through the quiet. He's still swaying slightly on his feet but his concern is more than genuine despite the alcohol that meant Lucas and I had to jump in just now.

"How are you feeling?" he asks me.

"I'm fine," I assure him, brushing back a loose strand of hair with a shaky hand. I said too much to Lucas before all that. I almost let it slip how much I want a baby, not that that's a bad thing to want I guess...but if he knew I was already in the process of doing it alone...

Why do I suddenly care so much about what he thinks?

Around us, the remaining guests are murmuring their relief. Their faces are all lit by the soft glow of the lanterns strung above the now vacant rodeo ring. "We should probably get a cab back to the hotel," I suggest.

"Sorry, guys," Hank begins, steadying himself against a nearby post. "No taxis will come out here till morning now. Stay the night, whoever needs to! Rose, Lucas, you're the heroes of the hour. I have rooms all made up in the guesthouse."

Oh. "No taxis?" I look to Lucas, searching for any sign of his own discomfort. His deep brown eyes give nothing away.

"Appreciate it, Hank," he says. Then he turns to me. "He's right. That little situation took us past the cutoff point for cabs. We could stay and get a ride back first thing in the morning? At first light, if you want?"

Hank tells us there are toothbrushes, towels, lotions and even swimwear and robes in the drawers if we need them, and though I wasn't planning on this at all, I am kind of intrigued as to what the guesthouse might look like. Plus, the long ride back to the hotel sounds less appealing by the second. I'm exhausted.

"We'll take the rooms. Thank you," I say, just as a guy I recognize from the dinner table walks up to us and explains he has had one too many beers to drive, and so has his colleague.

Hank ushers us all toward a building in the direction of the pond. The guesthouse is a rustic little place with cedar walls that seem to blend into the surrounding greenery, and in the moonlight it looks like something out of a storybook. A carved wooden sign dangles from the eaves, engraved with the words *Eagle Lodge*.

The interior is simple but comfortable, filled with homey touches like a wood-burning fireplace and handmade quilts on the plush sofas. I look up at the ceilings with their authentic, old-fashioned wooden rafters. Then I see the giant taxidermy eagle, wings spread from its mount like it's about to take off.

"I feel like I just stepped into a movie set," I say to Lucas, and he snickers.

The guy from dinner and his colleague disappear down a hallway, leaving Lucas and me standing in the living room with Hank. "Well," Hank says, removing his hat and running a hand through his hair. "There's just one problem."

I stiffen, my heart pounding in my chest. Somehow, I know what he's going to say.

"I've only got the one room available now," Hank continues, oblivious to my horror. "You'll both have to share."

"I see," Lucas says without missing a beat. There's an unreadable look in his eyes as they flicker toward me in the dim light. "So, we're roommates, then?"

To his credit, Hank doesn't wink at Lucas or anything. He's still trying to remain upright by the looks of it. My mind reels as I look at Lucas, hoping for a way out of this predicament, but his expression is inscrutable. For reasons I can't quite articulate, the thought of sharing a bed with Lucas fills me with a growing sense of equal dread and excitement.

"No problem, Hank," he says, "I can take the couch."

Oh. Of course he'd take the couch. Why on earth did I think he would choose to share a bed with me, as if I would have agreed, anyway? Where is my mind at?

"I can sleep anywhere, trust me," he says, shrugging at me, and I sigh and tell him thanks.

"Night, folks. Rose, your room is through there." With another somewhat weary tip of his hat, Hank lumbers off toward his own quarters, leaving us alone.

Lucas drops to the couch and removes his hat again. I drop to another padded armchair, my fingers tracing the patterned upholstery. "Well, that was…intense."

"Yeah." Lucas rubs his temples and I watch his big hands move across his head. "But you were incredible out there. On the stage, at the rodeo in a crowd of drunken cowboys… What can't Rose Carter do, huh?"

There's a dreamy quality to his voice that's both tired and awestruck and I look away as my face heats up. "Team effort," I remind him. I can't exactly accept individual praise when it was our joint capabilities that made the difference to Ty.

"Still," he insists, "you've got this…poise under pressure."

"I guess I have to, living with toddlers," I quip, trying to deflect the compliment and his obvious admiration with humor. He's making me feel things I shouldn't be feeling, things I cannot afford to contemplate right now.

He nods, and his gaze is thoughtful, distant for a moment. For a second I am quite certain he's going to bring up something from our earlier conversation, when I as good as told him I've stayed single and pathetic, living with my sister and her children since my relationship failed. However, he merely grabs a few cushions and starts plumping them around his head with his fist before shaking off his chunky boots and lying horizontally on the couch. "Good night, Rose."

I stand as his yawn transfers to me. "Good night, Lucas."

The room is cozy enough, with warm hues of brown and orange splashed across the wallpaper, embroidered horse pillows and vintage cowboy hats hanging on brass hooks, but for some reason, I can't sleep at all. I rustle the cowboy-themed linens as I toss and turn on the bed, trying to ignore the ringing silence and the fresh rush of anxiety I can't quite place. It's been such an eventful day. And Lucas is on the other side of the wall. It's the closest I've been to a sleeping man in a long, long time, and I can't get our conversations out of my head, or the feeling that he might feel a slice of this attraction, too. He even invited me to go on some kind of urban adventure with him, as if I ever would!

Why wouldn't I?

I don't actually know. I don't know what these feelings are all of a sudden.

My eyes catch the wooden dresser in the corner of the room. Curious, I rise from the bed and open the first drawer to find an assortment of neatly folded clothes—plaid shirts, jeans, even a fringed suede jacket. It looks like an entire cowboy wardrobe. I smile to myself—Hank really has thought of everything. The second drawer presents another surprise—the swimwear he mentioned. I roll my eyes at several bikinis in various colors and patterns that wouldn't look out of place on a beach in California, along with matching sarongs and beach towels. A soft, fluffy robe lies on top in a deep shade of blue.

I hesitate for a moment before pulling out one bikini—a simple yet elegant black two-piece—alongside the blue robe, which feels invitingly soft. Well, why not? Slipping into the swimwear makes me realize how long it's been since I last enjoyed an unplanned moonlit activity like this, but the pond outside is calling me now.

Wrapping myself tightly in the robe, I step out through the back door onto the porch. The ranch is quiet. Only the chirping crickets and a distant hoot of an owl reach my ears. The moonlight bathes everything in its silvery glow as I step toward the pond, only to find there's someone else in the water.

CHAPTER SEVEN

I PUSH MY body through the water, focusing on each stroke that slices the pond's surface while my heart thuds against my rib cage. I thought I was exhausted but the adrenaline is still surging through me, from both the incident with Ty and…her. I needed to swim off my thoughts about Rose. It was killing me, knowing she was sleeping just beyond those wooden walls.

I insisted she take the bedroom, playing the gentleman of course, while I took the couch. It was the right thing to do, but damn if being that close wasn't testing my self-control. Her green eyes seem to linger in my thoughts like an unshakable melody lately—they have done since the moment we met, but she's getting to me even more after today.

I shared too much about my life, too much about my hobbies, my love of sneaking into abandoned buildings with my internet friends. Mabinty hated me doing it. Rose probably thinks I'm crazy, too, or stupid, or both. At least the fact that I never once left the table to mingle tonight meant I avoided talking about Mabs with anyone else who knew us as a couple. I still feel so damn guilty whenever someone mentions her name.

How was Ayden supposed to know I broke things off months ago? I told him tonight, but no one knows it ended in my heart long before I grew the balls to end it in person. How do you tell your childhood best friend, teenage lover and adult partner all rolled into one that you just don't see a future together? That the thought of bringing babies into the world together makes you want to run a mile?

Above, a dome of stars shines over me, brighter than anything I ever saw in NY or Chicago. My mind runs over Rose on that stage earlier; she looked amazing. She's hot, she knows how to command a room, but whereas many women like her would have an ego the size of one of Hank's hay bales, she's got this calming energy about her that's nice to be around. And she's divorced. I wonder what that David guy did. Whatever it was, he's an idiot.

A rustle from the sidelines makes me stop in my tracks. My feet find the pond's squishy, slippery bottom and my muscles tense, ready for anything—anything except her.

"Sorry, didn't mean to startle you." Rose is looking at me almost sheepishly from the cool grass, standing there wrapped in a dark blue robe. "Looks like we had the same idea."

"Great minds," I quip, keeping my tone light, my position strategic. The dark waters are my ally now. They are hiding my current naked status. With her in the bedroom, I didn't have easy access to swimwear or a robe, and I didn't exactly expect anyone else to be out here.

"I hope you don't mind?" she says, but there's no real question for me to answer. She's already unfastening the soft belt from around her middle. I watch it slide from her slender shoulders to the ground.

"Not at all," I manage. My voice comes a shade rougher than intended. "The water's perfect."

I swallow a groan, sinking lower into the pond. Here she is, moonlight dancing on her skin, clad in a bikini that leaves little to the imagination. I force my gaze upward, toward the endless starry sky and the full white moon as she slips into the water, but it's no use. Every cell in my body is acutely aware of her presence and how little she is wearing, and the fact that I am wearing absolutely nothing.

Get a grip, Lucas. I swim to the opposite side of the pond, putting some distance between us. I can feel her watching me, her curious gaze like a physical touch on my skin.

"Sorry again," she says finally, breaking the

silence. "I couldn't sleep, and I really didn't know you were out here."

"It's okay," I reply automatically. "I couldn't sleep, either."

We are both quiet for a moment, just floating in the water.

"You know," she says suddenly. "I can't believe I've never been on an actual ranch before."

I chuckle softly, grateful for her light tone. It makes a little of the awkwardness melt away, at least. "What do you think so far?"

"It's beautiful," she answers sincerely, spinning slowly in the water to take in the night sky above us. "And peaceful."

"That's one of the things I love most about it," I admit. "That and the peach cobbler."

She smiles. "That was divine. But really, I can see why he swapped the city for a place like this."

"Uh-huh." I can't seem to find any more words. Should I tell her I'm completely bare under these deceiving ripples? No. I let the secret sit heavy between us. Something else is growing by the second now, too, seeing her in this bikini. I need to say something.

"So...you said you were married once?"

Great, Lucas. That's not going to make things awkward at all.

She pauses, the water around her stilling as if awaiting her response.

"Sorry, I didn't mean to pry," I say, my words

quick. "That must have come out of left field, but it's been on my mind since you said it. I know I kinda cut you off myself back there at the table, when we touched on relationship stuff."

"You said you didn't want to talk about it," she replies, floating onto her back, causing her breasts to stick out of the water and taunt me.

"I did say that." I smirk. "So I don't expect you to talk about it, either. Forget I asked."

"It's okay." Her sigh is laced with a weary kind of acceptance. "I was married once, yes—to a surgeon. Met him during my residency. We lasted eight years, before he cheated."

Her openness surprises me and her honesty pulls at something in my chest. I can almost sense the things she's not saying about her surgeon, and empathy makes me move a little closer before I remember my naked state. I move away again.

"I'm sorry to hear that," I tell her. "And I can't believe any man in his right mind would divorce you."

The words are out before I can help it and she smiles to herself, but I can see she's embarrassed.

"So, were you ever married to Mabinty?" she asks, turning the spotlight on me.

Her name from Rose's mouth is jarring, but I shake my head.

"No." I swim around her carefully as she looks at the sky. "We were together a long time, but it never got to that point."

We continue to float. The silence now is loaded despite a roar from the cicadas. She's making a conscious effort not to float too close, not to touch me at all. I feel like she's waiting for me to talk more, and I wouldn't usually; I had no intention of even bringing it up... But something about the way she let me talk so easily earlier at the dinner table, and how great it felt to have her listen, makes the words fall out of me.

"Mabinty and I, we go way back," I start. "Since we were kids."

She turns to me. "Really? How did you guys meet?"

"She was playing soccer with some of her friends and I was just walking by when she kicked the ball a little too hard. It ended up hitting me right in the face. I cried."

"You *cried*?"

"I was eight, it hurt."

She laughs, covering her mouth before settling back into the water. "What an introduction."

"Yeah," I agree with a smile. "But that's what started our parents talking. They're from Sierra Leone." I pause a minute as the flashbacks hit me, how I'd be so excited when my father finally dropped his work to spend an hour or two just being a dad, and a husband and friend, only to watch him play the part and then go right back to his study and close the door on me.

"My parents went there once on one of Dad's

business trips, a West Africa trip. I don't know… they just clicked over the connection, I guess," I continue. Rose doesn't need to know the details of how I was left with the nanny, how I begged and begged to be allowed to go, just to spend more time with my father outside the house.

"It grew into dinners and meetups for them, play dates for me and Mabs. We grew up together and then when we turned fifteen or sixteen…"

"It grew into more. That's so cute. Sounds like you two had a great relationship," she says, almost wistfully.

"We did," I reply, trying not to let my emotions get the best of me. The arguments toward the end were anything but cute. Mabinty couldn't understand my reasons for not wanting kids, because I had trouble articulating why that was, exactly. I work as hard as my father did now—a way of maintaining control of my life, I guess, and maybe if I'm honest, avoiding the chaos and emotional vulnerability that comes with parenthood. I've spent my whole life trying to justify why my dad was the way he was…why he had a kid, only to ignore him for the most part, but who knows how I'd handle having kids myself? Maybe they'd annoy the crap out of me, too. Maybe I'd also prefer to focus on my work forever. "Sometimes things just don't work out," I say.

"I know all about that," she says softly. "So, what happened?"

"She wanted to start a family," I hear myself say. The admission hangs heavy between us. "And I realized I didn't."

I glance at Rose. She's frowning slightly at the sky, like the moon just did something to upset her, and my mind flashes back again; this time to the doomed Dubai trip, the last trip I took with Mabs. The tears in that hotel room when I finally blurted out that we needed to break up for good. I didn't tell her that not only did I not want kids, I had also fallen out of love with her. How could I have told her what I knew would hurt her more?

"We were kids when we met, you know?" I say. "The two of us just…started wanting different things."

Rose turns to me, her gaze steady. "What do *you* want?"

Her question hangs in the air, bold and direct, almost like a challenge. I take a breath. "Honestly? I'm not sure."

She watches me, waiting, and I feel this pull to keep going, even though the truth is messier than I'd like to admit. "There was always this understanding with Mabs. Like, we'd become parents someday. But it felt so far away, something for the future. And then suddenly, that future was right now, and I just—" I pause, struggling for the words. "I couldn't do it. I didn't want it."

Rose is still staring thoughtfully at the moon.

"So, what happened? You ended it because of that?"

"It wasn't just that," I say, my voice dropping. "It was like, if I couldn't be the man who wanted the same things she did, then I didn't even know who I was anymore. I'd spent so long picturing this future with her, and when that fell apart, I kind of...fell apart, too. I also felt heartless, which I hate."

She looks at me, her frown deepening. "It doesn't make you heartless to admit something isn't right for you."

I glance away. Am I saying too much? She's so easy to talk to. "Sometimes it feels like it, though. Like I let her down."

Rose shakes her head. "I think it makes you honest. And brave, actually. You only get one life. You walked away from something that wasn't working."

I let her words settle over me, along with the weight of them. "I don't know about *brave*. I'm still figuring out who I am, what I want...after spending so long thinking fatherhood was just this obligation waiting to happen."

She tilts her head. "Maybe it's not about knowing exactly what you want yet. Maybe it's just about being open enough to figure it out."

I smile back as a strange sense of calm washes over me. "You are so wise. How did you get this wise?"

"I watched a lot of Oprah," she says with a smile.

I go on to explain that while Mabs and I were the picture of a perfect couple who knew each other inside out, cracks had started to appear years before it all blew up. Behind closed doors we were barely together. All the nights she spent in the lounge drinking basil-infused cocktails with her egomaniac tech friends, while I pored over new medical studies in a different corner of the house, using earplugs so as not to hear their insufferable music. My fascination with the intricate world of genetics was more than an academic pursuit. It was my calling, my form of meditation. Like Rose's gardening. The millions of nucleotides holding the secrets of life was a world that mystified and enthralled me as much as my urban escape adventures, and Mabs didn't understand any of it. Nor did she really care.

I tell her how Mabinty went full speed into tech development while I was consumed by my medical studies. She helped launch several startups, even built an app that ended up trending. By our late twenties our lives had started to diverge completely, but we kept pretending everything was okay. We went out for ice cream as we always did, spent weekends playing board games or hiking in the mountains, yet the connection was fading. Our core differences grated on me for so long before I spoke up and broke her heart.

"Did you ever want kids, before your divorce?" I ask Rose. We've been talking so long now my fingers are shriveled but I don't care.

Her breath catches, and she looks away, her hands tracing patterns on the water's surface to her sides. "David and I were trying for a baby," she confesses. "That's when I found out about his affair."

"While you were trying for a baby?" My heart clenches. Instinctively, I move to comfort her, but then I halt.

Boundaries, Lucas, I remind myself.

"How long ago did this happen?"

"Six years ago."

We're quiet for a moment, processing. This guy really is an idiot.

"I ended things with Mabs six months ago," I tell her. "And you were right before. It *is* the biggest reason I left New York. I thought it would make things easier for both of us. And when the role at Evergreen came up... I just went for it."

"Are you still in touch?"

"Not really. We made a clean break," I say. "It was for the best."

Rose nods slowly. "Sorry," she mutters as if she's coming out of a daze. "I didn't mean for us to get that...personal."

"Well, neither did I, but here we are," I reply, and I meet her gaze, just as I realize I have drifted close enough to touch her, and she hasn't moved away. "Just two people in a fishpond, baring their souls."

She huffs a laugh, then puts her feet to the bottom.

"There aren't any fish in here, are there?" she says next, looking around her warily.

Now it's my turn to laugh. I'm less than a foot from her now. My fingers itch to reach out and confirm she's as real as she is raw and beautiful. This attraction is crazy; the way we can talk is so…different. I feel strangely, emotionally connected to this woman in a way I can't go back from now, and I'm pretty sure she feels it, too.

Our knees touch just for a second before I pull away and dunk under the water, needing to reset myself. I said I wouldn't do this, and she'd think even worse of me if I hit on her now, right after telling her everything about Mabinty. I'm not that guy. At least I don't want to be.

When I emerge from the water, Rose has swum to the shore. She climbs out and pulls the robe back around her, leaving me naked and alone once again. "I should at least go try to get some sleep before the sun comes up," she says, tying the belt around her waist with a definitive knot.

"Good night again," I say.

"Good night again," she says with a smile. She turns to go and right as I'm about to follow her in all my nakedness, she spins back around and I'm forced to duck back under the water. "Thanks for tonight," she says. "You have no idea how much I needed it."

CHAPTER EIGHT

THE MOMENT THIRTY-FIVE-YEAR-OLD brunette Sarah walks into my consultation room, I can sense her anxiety. She fidgets with her wedding ring and her glasses, and her eyes dart around nervously. I offer a reassuring smile as I gesture for her to take a seat.

"I'm fine, Doctor Carter," she says, when I ask her how she is. Then she lets out an aggravated gurgling sound before pressing her palms to the desk between us. "Okay, I'm lying. I'm nervous as hell. I… We've been trying for so long. So many times a week…sometimes several times a night, and nothing. What is wrong with me?"

I bite back a smile. This is not uncommon. Women always open up to me about this stuff. My heart aches for her, though, the second her eyes cloud over, and I feel instantly guilty that when she alluded to all the sex she's having, I started thinking yet again about Lucas. I haven't stopped thinking about him since that night in the pond two weeks ago, though I need to, badly.

He is no match for me, despite every atom in my body reminding me our chemistry is off the charts. Now he's not just a colleague, he's another man who doesn't want a family. Not a good match, Rose!

As Sarah tells me about her journey into attempted motherhood, I jot down notes. Eighteen months of trying. Multiple negative pregnancy tests. The same crushing disappointment each month when her steady cycle refuses to be disrupted, despite keeping close tabs on it and having a very enthusiastic partner.

It's a familiar story, one that resonates deeply in my bones. I haven't been having any sex, obviously, much to Lily's chagrin—she wants nothing more than to see me coupled up again, or at least out having "fun"—but it's not like I haven't been doing my best to prepare my body for the art of growing and carrying a child.

I have been eating all the right things and not drinking all the wrong things, with the exception of that one night off in Texas two weeks ago. I've been doing yoga with Lily, taking folic acid, vitamin D, omega-3 fatty acids, spiritual advice from podcast hosts. Yet, according to my doctor across town, with whom I sat just yesterday, I am still not pregnant. The test was negative. I'm no closer to becoming the ideal sanctuary necessary to host a living being than I was this time last year. But I'm doing my best not to dwell. I'm keeping busy.

"We'll start with some basic tests," I explain to Sarah, leaning forward. "Hormone levels, ultrasounds, the tubes test. For your husband, we'll do a sperm analysis. Is he here?"

She scowls. "He says the problem isn't him."

That's what they all say. I almost tell her this, but of course I don't. Sarah's shoulders relax slightly. "We can arrange that," I say instead.

I walk her through each option that we might explore down the line, from medication to stimulate ovulation, to IUI or IVF, watching as hope slowly replaces the fear in her eyes. It's moments like these that remind me why I chose this field. Why I come here every day and help all these women, even though I still can't help myself. Why was my test negative, *again*? They're running more tests. I'm on more meds. Same story as before. I feel like I'm stuck in a loop, going nowhere.

As I schedule Sarah's first round of tests, my mind drifts again to Lucas. The sound of his voice, his laugh, everything he said about Mabinty, everything I said about David. I haven't opened up like that to anyone in a long time; nobody except Lily. It felt so freeing somehow. And I can't stop thinking about him now.

Dammit. I need to stop this!

The second Sarah's gone with armfuls of information and restored hope, and a planned stern talk with her husband about his sperm, Lucas's head pops around the door. He looks excited and my heart rate spikes. "Good news about Emily Hanson," he says, stepping into the room. "She's pregnant. She just called to say she did a test. She's on the way in."

I feel my mouth fall open for a second, before I remember to paste on a smile. "That's fantastic," I say, hoping my voice sounds genuinely excited. Of course, this is fantastic news. She's only been on the estrogen for a couple of weeks! She's been sticking to Lucas's revised treatment plan, too, and apparently, it's worked.

Lucas's eyebrows furrow slightly. "You okay?"

"Everything is great," I lie, shuffling papers on my desk. I'm having to force down the bitter taste of envy suddenly, and the fact that the second he's close to me, my own hormone levels do their best to prove they're not faulty in any way whatsoever. They are far from perfect. My body stubbornly resists every treatment I've tried. But I can't tell Lucas that. I'd feel so embarrassed. Already this is complicated.

He's still looking at me in suspicion as he pretends to leaf through a file.

"Such good news for Emily. She must be thrilled," I add quickly. "No doubt your amended plan had something to do with it."

Lucas's dark eyes search my face, his expression softening with concern. "Are you sure nothing's wrong? You seem...off."

His gaze reminds me of that night in Texas, the way he looked at me under the stars, and I feel a flutter in my stomach. I squash it immediately and wave away his words. He opens his mouth as if to press me further, but his eyes suddenly shift to something behind me.

"Wow. Those are something else. I'm surprised you don't have a swarm of bees and butterflies in here with *that* dominating the space."

I turn to follow his gaze toward the massive bouquet on the windowsill. I know what he means. It's a completely over-the-top, beautiful-smelling and brightly colored riot of sunflowers, daisies and bluebonnets. It is, in fact, a distinctly Texan arrangement.

"They're something else indeed," I say. "Ty sent them as a thank-you for helping him out after that unfortunate bucking bronco incident."

Lucas's eyebrows rise slightly. "Ty?"

Is it my imagination, or does he sound a little jealous?

"Yes," I reply, keeping my tone casual. "He wanted to show his appreciation. It was a nice gesture."

Lucas nods, his expression unreadable. "Very nice." His voice is carefully neutral. Then he grins, his white teeth flashing against his dark skin as he steps farther into the room, closing the door behind him. The soft click of the latch sends my heart racing harder, and I silently chide myself for this involuntary reaction. I shouldn't feel this way in his presence. This is how I started feeling around David in our early days, before we started sneaking into store cupboards to make out…before he decided our entire relationship and marriage was a disposable object he could have his fill of, then toss into the trash like a chewed-up apple core, leaving me floating round the halls like a ghost of myself, terrified of bumping into him.

"Speaking of Ty," Lucas says, pulling out his phone, "look at what he sent *me*."

"He sent you something, too?"

"*Something* is the word." He holds up the screen, revealing a photo of an enormous gleaming belt buckle, even bigger than the one Hank was wearing that night. It's pure Texas kitsch—a silver longhorn skull surrounded by intricate rope work and studded with what looks like genuine turquoise stones. I mean, it's hideous.

I can't help but laugh. "Oh, my God, that's…"

"Ridiculous? Amazing? Both?" Lucas chuckles, his eyes crinkling at the corners. I like how his eyes smile.

"Definitely both," I agree, studying the gaudy accessory instead of him, despite the fact that it's getting harder every time I see him now. "I'm starting to think you dress like a rancher every day and we just don't know about it in here."

"Damn, my secret is out," he teases. "Well, now you know, why don't you come over to my place sometime and we can break it in properly? I'll make us some authentic Tex-Mex."

My stomach does a little flip, especially when he looks away to the floor, then scratches at his neck, like he's embarrassed that an invitation like that just slipped out of his mouth so spontaneously.

Unless he's been thinking about me since Texas, like I have been thinking about him.

I can't fight the small smile that finds my mouth as I catch his gaze again quickly, before we both look away and heat flames up my neck. I can't stop imagining him in that moonlit scenario, his cowboy shirt gone, bare skin glistening in the water. Droplets cascading down his chiseled face, merging with the pond, every muscle defined against his smooth, dark skin. His eyes are usually cheerful, if analytical, but they held a new layer of intensity under the moon that night we talked, and talked, and talked. I wanted him. That's why I had to force myself out of the water the second he dunked under. I can't have him.

Before I can formulate a response to his invite, a notification pops up on his screen, obscuring part of the belt buckle photo. It's Mabinty.

Hey, I'll be in Chicago in two weeks' time for a conference. Want to meet up?

A sudden chill snakes around me, as if someone's opened a window in the sealed room. Lucas's ex. The woman he was with for years, the one he wouldn't have children with. Why is she asking to meet him now?

My eyes flick up to his face, searching for a reaction. Whatever's going on, her timing is impeccable. He more or less just asked me out. At least, he asked me over to his house, to cook for me, which Lily will say is still classified as going out, because it's outside this hospital. I am way more flustered than I want to be.

"Are you going to see her?" I ask, trying to keep my voice neutral.

Lucas blinks, running a hand over his short, cropped hair. The mood has darkened now. He's probably forgotten that little moment we just shared. "I don't know. She still has some of my things at her place in New York. It might be a good opportunity to get them back, at least."

"What kind of things? She's not exactly going to drive here in a removal van and deliver your antique couch, is she?"

He grunts a laugh and I curse myself for the way that just sounded. I sounded like a jealous idiot. Jealous and cold, great. I don't trust myself to speak now. I'm too grouchy and emotional after the news about myself and selfishly, the news about Emily. It's not my business if he sees her on not. And yet, I can't help the overwhelming rush of envy I feel coming at me from every direction.

My pager tells me Emily and her husband, Nathaniel, have arrived, and I really have to psyche myself up. I can feel Lucas's presence beside me as we walk, even when he says nothing. That message from his ex is on his mind now, I can tell. Was it just one of many she's sent him since the breakup?

I remember how David hounded me before we finalized the divorce. He was more concerned about me damaging his reputation in the industry than he was about destroying our marriage. The fact that we'd been trying to get pregnant while he'd been screwing someone else seemed to elude him. I often wonder if he ever wanted it as much as I did, if my longing for motherhood was what caused his eye to wander in the first place. Lily hypothesized that he probably saw fatherhood as the end to all his fun, the nail in the coffin of what was left of his free time, and he just didn't know how to say it. Instead, he made a statement by pursuing someone else, forcing *me* to leave *him*. Coward.

Is Lucas like that, too? He doesn't seem anything like David.

Emily sits nervously in the chair opposite me,

her fingers twisting in her lap, hope and anxiety battling for dominance on her face as her husband takes her hand. I explain how we'll do the ultrasound, and then, when she's on the table and the grainy black-and-white screen confirms she is indeed, somewhat miraculously in my opinion, pregnant, I watch Emily's face. The joy, the hope, the excitement—it's all there, shining in her eyes. It's everything I've dreamed of feeling myself, everything I've longed for. I watch Nathaniel, too. He seems elated. I used to long to see that look on David's face.

"Do you have any more questions, Emily?" I ask her, once I've explained what happens now, the scan appointments, the follow-up tests. She shakes her head, still beaming. "No, I... I'm just so happy. Thank you both so much. We are over the moon."

I answer all her questions as best I can. She's concerned the pregnancy won't reach full-term, of course, but I assure her we'll be here every step of the way, while a new heaviness settles in my chest. Everyone seems to be getting their chance at happiness. Lily with her wedding fast approaching. Emily with her pregnancy, Lucas potentially reconciling with Mabinty...

The thought of that upsets me far more than it should.

"That guy Nathaniel is gonna be a great dad," Lucas says when they've gone, interrupting my spiraling thoughts. "You know when you can just tell?"

"How?" I hear myself ask him, distracted.

"They're both already so invested. That's a good start, trust me."

There's something in his tone, a hint at a darkness I don't think I've ever heard from him except for our conversation in the pond, and when he talks about his relationship with his dad. That's affected him more than even he lets on. I watch him making notes in their file. I'm distracted again, this time by his handwriting. Neat and clear, precise and deliberate. There's a sense of order and clarity that I wish I felt inside. Instead, I just feel like I'm unraveling. Am I not a family person? Do *I* need a family, as in, a husband to do this? Can I even keep going through all this on my own, all this heartbreak? What if I just can't have children?

I force a smile when I see him look up. "Sorry, what did you say? I'm a little—"

Oh, no. Maybe I should start accepting the fact that I'm probably not built to have babies in any way, shape or form. Maybe I just can't have kids, full stop.

I think I'm having a panic attack. Oh, no, *no, no*, this is no good.

"Excuse me," I manage, just as my chin wobbles. He looks at me in alarm as I cover my face and hurry from the room, and he calls something out but I don't stop. I rush to the nearest empty room, barely making it inside before the tears begin to fall. I heave deep breaths into my lungs, trying to calm myself down. This isn't professional at all, but it also isn't fair. Why do I have to struggle as a single divorcée while everyone around me seems to be either getting pregnant at the drop of a hat, or getting the good news I so desperately want to hear? It's not fair.

I wipe my face, press my hands to the basin in the corner, then sink to the bed to try to compose myself, but the floodgates have opened and I can't seem to stop crying now. I feel like such a failure—as a woman, as an ex-wife, as a doctor. How am I supposed to go on helping others when I can't even help myself?

I am still trying to collect myself when there's a soft knock on the door. "Doctor Carter? Are you all right?" It's Lucas's voice, so full of concern now it makes my eyes pool with a fresh wave of self-pity.

"I'm fine," I call out to him, swiping at my face, trying to sound convincing. I know I keep telling him this when I probably sound anything but. He's not an idiot. I scramble for my phone to buzz Lily but it's not in my pocket. I left it on the desk. Sucking in a breath I unlock the door. It opens and Lucas steps in. He looks at me with worry etched all over his handsome face and it only makes more tears well up in my eyes.

"You don't look fine," he comments, shutting the door again behind him.

I shake my head and let out another sob. "I'm just... I'm so sorry."

Lucas steps closer. For a long moment, or so it feels, he looks like he doesn't know quite what to do with me. Then to my total shock he wraps his arms around me and against every ounce of my professional demeanor, I lean into it. "It's okay," he says softly. "I'm here, Rose."

His chest is hard under my cheek, a wall of warm human strength. I allow myself to be cradled in his strong, safe arms, nestled against his heart, which is beating now, fast, hard, like mine. In this moment with Lucas holding me tight, and without me saying a word, all my emotions come pouring out—the frustration, the sadness, the anger...all of it. It feels like I'm emptying my soul in the silence, and he's just soaking it all up. I needed this.

"I'm not usually so emotional," I mumble, my voice muffled against him. "I don't know what's wrong with me. Well, actually, I do. I can't—"

"What is it?" His hand lingers on my back and I let out a shaky laugh, tearing up again, swallowing hard. The thought is too painful to voice out loud.

"Can't what?" Lucas asks gently, stepping back to look at me more closely.

"I can't have kids," I finally blurt out. The

words hang heavy in the small white room. "I don't think so, anyway."

"Oh," Lucas says softly, understanding washing over his face. He looks at me for a moment longer before his gaze drops to the floor and he nods slowly, understanding dawning in his eyes.

"I'm so sorry," he murmurs at last. "I didn't know." There's an apology in his voice and I'm taken aback by the sincerity there.

"How would you?"

"Well, we talked…in the pond."

"I wasn't just going to come out and say it, was I?"

"Okay." He nods, but I can see him processing. "You know this for sure?"

I shrug. "Not one hundred percent, no. It's just looking likely right now. Ironic, huh?"

Lucas looks like he wants to say something more but instead he takes a step forward and reaches out to gently brush my hair back from my face. His touch is soft, almost tentative, as if he's worried I might shatter into pieces any second. As if sensing my surprise, he quickly pulls his hand back, reaches for the dispenser and pulls more paper towels out. He hands them over, and puts his hands to my shoulders gently as I dab at my eyes.

"Do you want to talk about it now?"

I shake my head resolutely. The last thing I

want is pity from anyone, especially Lucas. "No, thank you. I just need…"

"Go home," he tells me. "I'll cover for you. Go home, make a big hot cup of tea and don't think about coming back until you've taken all the time you need."

I sigh. I can still feel the trace of his fingers on my skin. "Okay."

He peers down at me over his glasses. "Doctor's orders."

"Fine, thank you."

I don't understand why I just told him that; it just felt like I could, or should. I don't know a thing about what's going on in that head of his but somehow he has the power to get into mine, and I don't know what to do with it at all.

CHAPTER NINE

I SET THE grocery bags on the kitchen island, the rustle of paper echoing through the loft. Floor-to-ceiling windows frame the glittering Chicago skyline beyond my grand piano, but my mind is far from the view. Rose's words replay in my head as I swing open the refrigerator.

I can't have kids.

It's a complete surprise knowing all this now, considering how long we spent talking in Texas, but she must have her reasons for not telling me.

The organic kale crunches as I stuff it into the crisper drawer. Should I call her? Check how she's doing? It's only 6:30 p.m. She'll be home. I told her to rest. My fingers hover over my phone, hesitating.

A notification pings. It's not Rose. It's Mabinty.

Lucas, I know you said no, but please reconsider meeting me when I'm in town. I miss talking to you.

I sigh, sliding a carton of almond milk onto a glass shelf. Mabinty's coming for that tech conference. I think she's showcasing her fertility-tracking app. Ironic, given our history, or maybe not. She asked me years ago what kind of app I thought she should develop to help the most people, and this was the first thing I thought of.

The app's good, I'll give her that. Uses AI to predict optimal conception windows, integrates with smart devices. But seeing her? That's a minefield I'm not particularly ready to navigate again, even if she does want to bring me my collection of records and my vintage record player. I miss that thing; it's the only thing Dad ever gave me from his heart, instead of out of duty. I left them behind in my haste to leave New York. They're sitting in her Upper East Side apartment, collecting dust. I choose records over TV any day, but music doesn't sound the same from a stereo as it does from that old record player.

I reach for an apple, pressing my palm around its cool skin. Rose's face flashes into my mind again, the way her green eyes clouded over. Heartbreaking. I pulled her into me on autopilot, couldn't help it. My chest tightens. I didn't ask her anything more, like who is she trying for a baby with? Is she doing it alone, at a clinic somewhere else? How long has she been on this journey? I have a thousand questions now, but really, I just hope she's all right.

I want to text her and ask how she's doing. But is that overstepping? We're colleagues, nothing more. Even if I can't stop thinking about her.

The phone feels heavy in my hand. Mabinty's message glows accusingly. Rose's number tempts me. This is not an ideal situation. I take a bite of the apple, its tartness barely registering. What the hell am I supposed to do?

I settle on the couch, balancing a bowl of quinoa salad on my lap. I can't keep leaving Mabinty hanging, and the guilt gnaws at me even as I type out a response to her. I want my records back. But I have to do what's best.

I appreciate you reaching out, but I don't think meeting up is a good idea. Take care at the conference.

Send. Done. But the unease lingers. She doesn't just want to give me my records back; she wants to talk about what went wrong. She wants to ask me again why I suddenly decided I didn't want kids. She wants to remind me I'm not my father—of course she knows how my father barely looked at me when we were living in the same house—and then we'll fight and wind up in exactly the same place we are in now, because I never could find the courage to tell her how I fell out of love with her, and that *that's* the overarching reason why I wouldn't have *her* kids. I guess I've never thought about having a family with anyone else; I've never really let that sit. It was always gonna be me and Mabs, or no one.

Until I held Rose in my arms. She sends my brain to strange territories.

My thumb hovers over Rose's contact. Before I can overthink another situation, I start typing:

Hey, Rose, how are you doing?

The dots appear almost immediately. My heart rate picks up.

I'm OK. Sorry about earlier. I shouldn't have unloaded on you like that. I'm embarrassed.

No need to apologize.

Thanks, I appreciate that.

I put my bowl down on the coffee table, bring my phone closer.

Hope you're doing something fun to take your mind off things?

Oh, yes, absolutely. Having a blast.

I frown, sensing the sarcasm. What could she be up to? I know I should leave it here, but I'm enjoying waiting for her messages, knowing she's home but still talking to me. Knowing in some way I'm making her feel better.

Intriguing. Care to share?

She types again for a while, stopping and starting, and I realize I am fixated on the screen, waiting like an addict till her message appears.

I'm knee-deep in my sister's kids' finger-paint masterpiece. It's everywhere. Including my hair.

I can't help but grin to myself, picturing Dr. Rose Carter—always so put together at work—covered in rainbow splatters. Besides never feeling like I'd do fatherhood justice, I haven't spent much time around kids. I kind of kept my distance when our friends all started popping them out. I guess I never really know how to *be* around kids, how to act. Like my father? His awkwardness extended to me and there's no base to it, really; it's just how it is, how it's always been.

My only involvement with children and babies so far has been helping other people conceive them, which a psychologist would have a field day with, I'm sure. Lucas Bennett, bringing kids into the world so parents can love them, in all the ways *he* wasn't.

I type back.

Sounds like a real Picasso situation.

It really is. Thanks for checking in, Lucas. It means a lot.

I stare at her last message, warmth spreading through my chest. *It means a lot.* I like that. The quinoa salad sits forgotten on the table as I contemplate what to say next. Should I leave it there? Or…

My fingers hover over the keyboard. Indecision gnaws at me. The urban exploring event this weekend flashes through my mind—the abandoned Riverview Amusement Park just outside the city. It's been on my bucket list for ages. Exploring its decaying roller coasters and overgrown snack stands with the group, and Rose, would be fun. I'll bet she's never done anything like it.

But should I ask her? The rational part of my brain screams no. I'm her colleague, her ally. There are lines we shouldn't cross. She's trying for a baby! But I care about her now. She's snuck into a special place in my heart, and she needs something to lift her spirits, doesn't she?

Before I can talk myself out of it, I type.

Actually, I might have an idea to cheer you up. My urban exploring group is checking out the old Riverview Park on Sunday. Want to join? Promise it'll be more fun than finger painting.

I hit Send, my heart pounding. What am I doing? This is a terrible idea. I should follow up, tell her to forget it—

The three dots appear. My breath catches. They disappear. Reappear. Vanish again.

I stare at the screen as the silence stretches on. I cross to the piano, sit behind the keys. Each second feels like an eternity. What is she thinking? Is she trying to find a polite way to say no? Or worse, is she uncomfortable that I asked at all?

The dots pop up once more. I lean forward, gripping the phone so tightly my knuckles turn white.

My fingers hover over the phone's keyboard. I glance up at Lily, who's perched on the arm of the couch, peering over my shoulder while running her hands along their cat Jasper's silky back. He's purring so loudly I swear he has something to say about this situation.

"Well?" Lily prods. "Are you going to say yes or what? Don't keep him waiting!"

I chew my lower lip. "I don't know. It's complicated."

Theo, Lily's husband, looks up from where he's sprawled on the floor, building a tower of blocks with Harley and Amelia. He likes to tire them out mentally before bedtime. "Come on, Rose. When's the last time you did something spontaneous?"

I remind them how I borrowed a sexy bikini and took a moonlit dip in a pond a few weeks ago, which only wound up with me getting closer to Lucas than I should have, and then, as if on cue, one of the twins toddles over and plops a plastic dinosaur in my lap. "Rawr!" Amelia growls, grinning up at me.

I sigh through a smile, running my fingers through her cute curls. "You think I should go, too, huh?"

"Absolutely she does. Your niece is never wrong," Lily chimes in. "It's just an outing with a friend, anyway. No pressure, no expectations."

I let my fingers hover over the phone again. He knows now what a mess I am. He knows I'm trying for a baby and he must have a million questions about that, which I don't expect to get away with not answering for long. At least this adventure would give us a chance to talk properly again outside of work, and it's not like we'll be alone. He goes to these things in a group, he told me. Besides, he's probably getting back with his ex; he's only trying to be nice to a colleague in a new place he's never lived in before.

I let a small spark of excitement ignite in my chest. Exploring the old fairground sounds just the right amount of dangerous and risky to be fun. "You know what? You're right. I need to get out of my own head."

Then with a newfound determination, I type.

Count me in!

I hit Send before I can second-guess myself, even as anticipation flutters like a flock of sparrows in my stomach.

"There," I say, setting down my phone triumphantly. "I did it."

Lily lets out a whoop of joy, startling the twins, who giggle in response. "That's my flower girl!" she exclaims, pulling me into a tight hug. I fend her off; she's always so dramatic. "Invite him for dinner after? We're doing Theo's famous lasagna on Sunday."

"I'll get the good cheese," Theo promises.

"I'll think about it," I tell them, although there's absolutely no chance I'll be asking Lucas to dinner with this lot of crazy people. I shouldn't even be going to the abandoned park with him, all things considered, but…well, screw it. It's just one day out. What could go wrong?

CHAPTER TEN

I watch Rose's green eyes widen as she takes in the skeletal structure looming against the crisp blue sky. The rusted metal of the abandoned roller coaster is creaking slightly in the breeze, and she pulls out her phone to take a photo, smiling. I adore her smile.

"Incredible, isn't it?" I say, unable to keep the excitement from my voice now that we're here. The thrill of urban exploration never gets old, but sharing it with Rose today is adding a new dimension of exhilaration. I love when someone else seems to enjoy this stuff.

She nods, snapping another photo. "It's…beautiful, in a way."

I beam at her enthusiasm. "I'm glad you came, Rose. Not everyone appreciates places like this." I can't help thinking of Mabinty as I say it. She came with me precisely once, to an old abandoned prison, and wound up calling an Uber after ten minutes, deeming it cold and creepy, which it was, but that was the point.

We're standing at the edge of Riverside Park. This sprawling space was once a bustling fairground on Chicago's outskirts, but these days it's a ghost of its former self. Overgrown weeds are pushing through cracked concrete, and faded paint peels in all directions from derelict concession stands.

"I can picture it how it used to be," Rose says, narrowing her eyes as she looks around. "In fact, I think Dad brought me and Lily here when we were kids."

The rest of our group is clustered around the base of the roller coaster, snapping photos and debating its structural integrity. I gesture toward a quieter area of the park. "Do you want to explore over there?"

Rose nods, following me down a weed-choked path. The crunch of dead leaves under our feet fills the silence between us.

"So," I begin, keeping my tone casual despite the nerves fluttering in my stomach, "how are you feeling? After the other day, I mean."

Her shoulders tense slightly. "I'm fine. Work's been busy since I got back."

I nod, sensing her reluctance. "I know. And we haven't had a chance to talk about…you know, the baby thing."

Rose's pace slows, her gaze fixed on the ground. "Lucas, I—" she starts, then stops abruptly.

My heart rate quickens. I want to know more,

to understand what she's going through, but I don't want to push it. "You don't have to talk about it if you're not comfortable," I offer and she sighs, running a hand through her wavy brown hair.

"It's not that. It's just…complicated."

I sense she's nervous. We pause beside a rusted merry-go-round, looking together at the dull and chipped horses that were probably so vibrant and colorful back in their heyday. Rose traces a finger along one of the poles, lost in thought.

"These things are never straightforward," I say. "We should know."

She looks up at me. Her green eyes are filled with a mix of emotions I can't quite decipher now, and it makes me study her harder while I get a little lost in her gaze. "No, they're not," she agrees softly after a moment, pulling her eyes away.

I hesitate, then ask the question that's been nagging at me. "Forgive me for asking this, but why are you doing this alone?"

She laughs, but it's a hollow sound. Her fingers trace along the back of a horse and its saddle as she contemplates her answer. "I guess, after my divorce, I didn't think I'd find anyone in time. And honestly? I learned not to trust men." She grimaces as she says it, flicking her gaze to me. "No offense."

"Ouch," I say anyway, feigning offense.

Rose is usually so composed, but I can see how

deeply her ex-husband's betrayal has affected her. I want to tell her not all men are like that, but platitudes probably won't help, nor will they be appreciated. And I crushed Mabinty's dreams of being a mother, too, didn't I? Not by cheating, but still. The guilt still haunts me. I could have broken it off sooner, given her more time.

I listen as Rose describes her latest IVF attempt. She had more test results back this week. The embryo didn't implant, the same story as the first time it failed, a case of the uterine lining being too thin. "After all the hormones, the procedures…the fact that it failed again because of something so basic is just so frustrating. Maybe I'm just not cut out to carry a child."

"Don't say that," I tell her, leaning against the merry-go-round, being careful not to put too much weight on the aging structure. The weight of unspoken words hangs between us instead, and I find myself wishing I could do more, say more. An idea crosses my mind.

An ex-colleague of mine is starting a new trial that might help with Rose's exact issue. It's a novel approach, using platelet-rich plasma to improve endometrial receptivity. Early results have been promising, especially for women who've had previous implantation failures. He was supposed to present at the conference in Texas but something came up, otherwise she would've heard about it. I consider bringing it up, but wouldn't that be going a step too far with my colleague?

The idea plays in my head as we walk on, and I gesture toward a dilapidated fun house in the distance. "Want to check that out?"

Rose nods. "As long as there are no clowns in there. I hate clowns."

As we walk, I can't help it all spinning around in my head, like the carousel once did. The doctor in me wants to offer solutions, to bring up the trial, which I'm pretty sure could be done from Chicago, too, while the man in me, who is irrevocably attracted to this woman who's set on having a baby alone... Well, that's a complication I don't know what to do with.

"So, how did you..." I pause, not really sure how to frame it. We stop by the fun house. Its warped mirrors reflect our distorted images and Rose takes a deep breath, intercepting my question.

"I went with a sperm donor," she says.

I turn to her, surprised by the sudden admission. "Oh?" I keep my tone neutral. I don't want to spook her.

She nods, her eyes fixed on the cracked pavement beneath our feet now. "Lily went with me to choose. It was an interesting process."

"I'm sure it was," I say carefully, bending down to pick up a flier as it blows past. It's an old one, dated from the late nineties, and I show her it, before putting it in my pocket. I am genuinely curious to hear more about her donor process, even if a twinge of something like jealousy sparks in my chest as she continues.

"It's not exactly like shopping for groceries. You're looking at medical histories, hobbies, interests, physical traits. It's surreal, trying to pick the genetic makeup of your potential child from a catalog, like designing a new kitchen or something."

This is so wild, to be jealous of a guy I've never met. Who *Rose* has never met!

I listen and tell her I think she's brave as we venture inside the old fun house.

"You think I'm brave? Or are you just being nice because I said the same thing to you about breaking it off with your ex?"

I feel another twinge of guilt over telling Mabs I couldn't see her, but I forget it once she starts describing picking out the right "father" with Lily. I do think she's brave, but there's a part of me that's kind of angry on her behalf. She deserves someone amazing, someone who wants to build a family with her. Someone like me… except, that's not what I want. I'm single for the first time ever. I want to enjoy it! As soon as I find some time.

The scent of mildew greets us. Our warped reflections stretch and twist in more polished distortion mirrors lining the corridor.

"So, you definitely don't want kids of your own someday?" she says quietly, as if she's reading my mind. "Not even if Mabinty wanted to get back together?"

I frown at her. Why on earth would she think Mabs and I would get back together?

"Honestly? Growing up as an only child, I never really got the appeal of a big family," I tell her. "It was just me and my parents, and that always felt like enough."

Rose gives me a curious look. "Really? No part of you ever wanted siblings?"

I shrug. "Not really. I mean, I overheard them more than once saying how expensive I was. Like they could barely keep up with one kid, let alone more."

Her brow furrows. "Ouch. Did they really say that?"

"Yeah," I say, trying to keep it light. "They didn't mean for me to hear it, but as soon as I did, I couldn't help feeling like a bit of a burden. Like having kids was something they might've regretted."

She nods, scowling to herself. "That's heavy."

"Exactly," I agree, a little relieved that she gets it. "It's hard not to carry that around, you know? Thinking maybe you'll end up making someone else feel like that without even meaning to."

Rose looks at me, her gaze steady. "But that's

not who you are. Just because they felt that way doesn't mean you would."

I glance down, letting her words sink in. She has this strange way of making me contemplate things logically without me ever feeling judged. It's daunting, but refreshing, I guess.

I concentrate on carefully picking my way through the debris. The space looks strangely beautiful in its decay. Mirror shards catch stray sunbeams as they fracture light into fragmented rainbows across the dusty floor and she takes another photo, this time with me in it. Then, as if she's conjured it through her fear alone, a giant clown looms out at us in a button-up suit, and Rose shrieks, then trips on something in the darkness.

Laughing, I instinctively grasp her hand, offering a firm hold as we turn around the corner. Her fingers are cold but they warm up quickly in my grip. Looking down, she's laughing, but she mutters a bashful apology and attempts to let go. I hold on. Not only is the path unclear here, but our interlaced fingers feel more right than I ever imagined, like holding her felt the other day when she cried.

What is happening to me?

Then, a piercing scream cuts through the air, stopping us both in our tracks. My body reacts before my mind catches up. I'm already turning, running back the way we came toward the sound,

Rose right beside me. Her face is set in determination. All traces of our previous conversation have evaporated in the chilly air.

We round a corner of the dilapidated fairground. Rusted metal creaks under our feet as we enter an area with a no-entry sign on its gate. The source of the scream is getting clearer now: a young woman from our group, another newbie to the explorers who is maybe in her early twenties. She's sprawled at the base of a half-collapsed ticket booth.

The woman looks up as we approach and tell her we're doctors. Her face is pale and streaked with tears. "I... I was trying to get a better photo. The floor just gave way."

Rose is already kneeling beside her, her voice calm and reassuring. "I'm going to check you over, okay? Can you tell me your name?"

"Mia," the woman whimpers.

I scan the area, noting the jagged edges of the collapsed flooring. "Rose, watch out for any exposed nails or metal," I warn. The last thing I want is for her to get hurt, too.

She nods, her hands moving expertly over Mia's limbs. "Any pain when I touch here?" she asks, applying gentle pressure.

I crouch down on Mia's other side. "Mia, I need you to follow my finger with your eyes, all right?" I check for signs of concussion, my mind running through potential injuries. This is not the first time something like this has happened on one of these adventures, unfortunately, but these are the risks we take. I hope I haven't put Rose off for good; we had just stared to have fun, despite the serious talk, and the clown.

"Her right ankle's swollen," Rose reports. "Possible fracture or severe sprain. No obvious head trauma, but we should be cautious."

I agree, impressed by how quickly we've fallen into sync, like we did at the ranch that night. "Mia, we're going to help you up, but we need to move slowly. Any dizziness or nausea?"

Mia shakes her head, wincing as we carefully help her to a sitting position.

"Lucas," Rose says, her voice low. "We need to get her to a hospital for X-rays and a proper exam."

I nod, already pulling out my phone. "I'll call for an ambulance. Can you stay with her?"

Rose's hand on my arm stops me, her fingers digging into my biceps. "Wait. The hospital is at least thirty minutes away. We could drive her ourselves—it might be faster."

I hesitate, weighing the options. "You're right. Let's do it."

CHAPTER ELEVEN

THE HOSPITAL DOORS sweep open as Lucas and I rush Mia into the ER.

"Over here!" I guide Lucas, who's supporting Mia's weight. Her face is pale and her eyes are worryingly unfocused.

Theo, Lily's fiancé, emerges from behind a curtain, his expression shifting from surprise to concern in a heartbeat. "Rose? What happened?"

"Possible concussion, possible fracture or severe sprain to her right ankle," I explain quickly. "She fell during our…outing."

Theo's eyebrows rise slightly, but he's all business as he directs his staff. "Get her to bay three. I want a full workup—CT scan, the works."

As they whisk Mia away, the adrenaline roaring through my body starts to ebb but my hands are shaking. I hadn't realized how worked up I was until right now. I've been operating on autopilot. Lucas has been, too, I think. He sinks to a plastic chair and I sit beside him until Theo returns with his clipboard in hand. "She's in good hands. Thanks for bringing her in, guys."

"Thanks, Theo."

Theo glances at his watch. "Listen, I'm off in a couple of hours. Still on for dinner at the house tonight?"

I blink, momentarily thrown by the shift in topic. "Oh, right. Yes, of course."

Theo's gaze flicks to Lucas, then back to me. There's an expectant pause and I can literally feel the pressure building. Before I can overthink it, I blurt out, "Lucas, would you like to join us?"

Lucas looks surprised, then conflicted. "I wouldn't want to impose," he says slowly.

"You wouldn't be," I assure him, though part of me wonders if I'm making a mistake, pushing the topic when he really just doesn't want to come. I feel like I've fed him enough information today to warrant him running a mile. "It's lasagna," I hear myself say, anyway. "Award-winning, so Lily says. She's never elaborated on which award."

"Because it's a secret award she likes to give me in private," Theo says, deadpan with zero shame, and I screw up my face, tell him I didn't need to know that, and he laughs. He must have broken the ice because Lucas is smiling now. Finally, he nods.

"All right, then. Thank you. I'd love to join."

Theo looks pleased, of course. He knows exactly what he is doing here. "Excellent! I'll see you both later, then. Now, if you'll excuse me, I better get back to it."

I settle into the passenger seat of Lucas's car, my heart racing in a way that has nothing to do with the adrenaline from the ER or what just happened with poor Mia. The leather seat is cool against my back, and I draw a deep breath. I couldn't have *not* asked him to dinner, with Theo standing over us expectantly.

"That was wild, huh? Now, what's your address?"

He types the house address into his phone on the dash, and as we pull out of the hospital parking lot, my mind wanders back to our conversation earlier. I told him everything, and never once did it feel like he was judging me. In turn, he told me some stuff that hints at why he doesn't want kids...stuff that definitely stems from the way his parents were. And now I'm just conflicted. I think I am starting to want more. More than Lucas could ever give me, even if we didn't work together.

"I hope I didn't overshare earlier," I say, breaking the silence as we hit the freeway again. "About the donor and everything."

Lucas glances at me, his expression softening. "Not at all. You make me think that maybe..." He trails off, chewing his lip.

"What did I make you think about?" I ask him.

He shakes his head. "Never mind. Look, I can't show up to your place empty-handed. Mind if we make a quick stop?"

"Oh, of course not," I reply.

He pulls the car into a small shopping complex and parks. "I'll just grab a bottle of wine. Won't be a minute."

As he exits the car, I let out a breath I didn't realize I was holding. Being in an enclosed space with this man is starting to do strange things to my body and brain.

His phone buzzes on the dash, and I can't help seeing the message notification. It's from Mabinty. My stomach tightens as I read it.

I'll bring your record player. Just let me know where you want to meet.

Annoyance flares up from deep in my bones. So they *are* planning to meet.

Lucas slides back into the driver's seat, a brown paper bag in hand. "Got a nice Cabernet. I hope that's okay?"

I force a smile, pushing my thoughts about Mabinty aside. Why torture myself? "Perfect. Lily loves red wine."

He pulls a face. "You're not drinking. Right."

"It's all good," I tell him. "It's not like I'm pregnant." I can't help the way it comes out with a tone of defeat, and I roll my eyes when he turns to me. "Sorry, this must be so weird for you. I won't talk about it anymore."

He throws me a long look that tells me that it's all right, and also that there's something else he really wants to say, but doesn't know how. I question him with my eyes again, but again, he shakes his head and starts the car. My heart thuds all the way home.

The living room is a whirlwind of color and chaos as usual. Lily's started cooking and Lucas and I have settled in the lounge, where the twins are playing. Stuffed animals and building blocks litter the floor, and Lucas is sitting cross-legged amidst the mayhem with a purple feather boa draped around his neck. He's helping Harley stack a teetering tower of blocks. I can't say for sure, but it certainly seems like he's having a nice time, and it's a joy to watch them playing.

"Higher!" Amelia squeals at him, her chubby hands reaching for the sky.

Lucas grins, his earlier reservations nowhere to be seen. "Okay, but if it falls, we're blaming your aunt Rose."

I tut but I can't help the smile tugging at my lips. It's unexpected, seeing him so at ease with children. From what he was saying earlier, he hasn't really spent much time with them, and watching him now, a pang of longing hits me, sharp and bittersweet. How can I not imagine him as a father figure? But it's not what he wants. He broke up with his ex because of it, and now if anyone's going to change his mind, it's Mabinty, not me. Ugh, I need to curb this crush.

Lily emerges from the kitchen with a plate of apple slices. "Having fun, Lucas? I think the twins have found a new favorite playmate."

Before he can respond, the doorbell chimes. Theo's arrived. He has a key but out of respect he always rings the doorbell in case we're doing what he calls "lady things," whatever those are. As Lily goes to let him in and the twins reach for the apple slices, I catch Lucas's eye. He winks from within the feathers around his neck, and I feel the flush creep up my face. I busy myself with picking up some stray toys, trying to quell the butterflies in my stomach.

As usual, Theo runs upstairs to shower and when he emerges ten minutes later, his presence fills the room. The twins lunge at him, encircling his legs and waist with their little arms. "Good news," he says to me and Lucas, hauling Amelia into his arms. "Mia's been discharged. She's resting at home now, just a sprain, no lasting damage."

Lucas stands, carefully extricating himself from the sea of toys. "Well, that's good to hear. Though I'm afraid it means Rose will never want to go urban exploring with me again."

I feel my cheeks burn as he sits next to me on the couch, acutely aware of his presence beside me, in my home. "I think I've had enough excitement for one lifetime, thanks."

Lily, ever the instigator, pipes up, extracting three apple slices from Harley's fingers and replacing them with just one. "Oh, I don't know. Maybe you should keep asking her, Lucas. Who knows? She might surprise you."

I shoot my sister a look that clearly says *traitor*, but she just grins innocently and flicks her hair, curse her.

"I'll keep that in mind," Lucas says as Harley offers him the apple slice. His tone is light and even, but his brown eyes are a low level of intensity as they meet mine, and I have to look away. I busy myself with cleaning sticky fingers and making sure no apple slices get stuck between the sofa cushions.

Over dinner, once the twins are upstairs in bed, the conversation shifts to safer topics, thankfully. Lucas grins as he digs into the lasagna. "This is seriously good. Best I've had in ages."

Lily leans in. "So, Lucas, where did you grow up? How did you get into urban exploring? Have you ever—?"

I kick her under the table. "Lily!"

Lily just grins, turning back to Theo as they start their usual back-and-forth banter, half ignoring the rest of the table.

Lucas leans into me now, voice low. "So…if I haven't completely put you off, a few of us are planning to check out the Old Prairiewood Asylum in about a month. It's this abandoned place from the nineteen-thirties, meant for the criminally insane, way out by the Cook County Forest Preserves."

I feel my eyes widening. "You serious?"

Lucas smirks. "Dead serious. There might be a séance, too. Some of the girls in the group are into that."

"All right, you've got my attention. I'll think about it."

In truth, I would probably go if he asked me, but I don't want to appear too keen. Lily turns to us. Her eyes light up as she starts to discuss their upcoming wedding.

"So, we've been thinking about how to involve the twins," she says. "We want them to be part of the ceremony, but…"

Theo chuckles. "But we're not sure how to wrangle two energetic toddlers down the aisle."

I lean forward just as Lucas does, intrigued. "We need a plan."

Lucas's face breaks into a mischievous grin. "How about if you attach crates or baskets to a couple of cute ride-on toys. They can zoom down the aisle on them and scatter petals as they go."

The image makes me laugh. "That's brilliant."

He gives me a sideways smile and I catch Theo

and Lily looking at each other tellingly. "Speaking of the ceremony," I add quickly, "I'm auditioning three pianists early next month for the music."

As I speak, I notice Lucas looking at me even more intently. Our eyes meet, but Lily jumps in. "Lucas, don't you play?"

"How do you know I play piano?" he asks my sister.

My cheeks flame as Lily looks pointedly at me, then back to him. I'm going to murder her. She might as well come out and say that I've told her every single thing I know about him so far. Lily is shameless, though. "We wouldn't want you playing all night but maybe you could perform one piece at the wedding..."

"No pressure," Theo interrupts. "Obviously, we're inviting loads of staff from Evergreen, seeing as we wouldn't have met without them. It'd be so great to have a special piece from one of the staff who actually plays!"

Well, this is just fantastic. They're not so subtly trying to push us together at every given opportunity now. Lucas is never going to want to socialize with me anywhere again, let alone at their wedding.

"Guys, don't put poor Lucas on the spot," I say, attempting to change the subject. Thankfully, there's a scream from upstairs, and Theo excuses himself, quickly followed by Lily.

By the time they come back down we're making tea and talking about whether a séance is really likely to summon up any long-dead patients in an asylum on the outskirts of the city. Theo and Lily remain on their best behavior until finally, Lucas announces it's late and he has to go. I didn't even realize the time.

I walk him to his car, my heart racing in the cool night air. The silence between us feels charged now, like it always does when we find ourselves alone. He stops at the end of the driveway, turning to face me with his jacket in his arms. "I had a really nice time," he says. "The twins are great."

"They loved you," I say truthfully, and he nods, fixing his eyes on mine, which makes my heart start fluttering wildly. Then he lowers them down to my mouth, which makes it worse. This crush is irrevocable now. For a moment, I think he might actually kiss me, the way he's studying my lips. My breath catches and I feel my lust like a living thing, hot and hopeful in my throat. Maybe he wasn't scared off. But he also has that look on his face again, the one that tells me he wants to say something important and serious. He is going to address this attraction, I know it. He's not one to just kiss a woman, especially a colleague. He wants to talk about it first, and he knows by now that I'm not exactly the spontaneous type.

Or maybe he's going to announce that he and Mabinty are reassessing their relationship. I brace myself.

"Rose, there's something I wanted to mention," he starts, and I feel the prickles of anxiety start up my arms. I shouldn't do this... Look what happened with David; look how independent I've become ever since, how I've scraped myself back up from rock bottom to the point where I'm ready to be a mother, all by myself. I shouldn't. But oh, I want to...

"I wasn't sure whether to bring it up," he starts as I find myself inching closer. "But I actually know someone conducting a trial that might interest you. It might help your cause. Doctor Mei-Ling Tan."

Oh.

I root my feet to the street as Lucas continues telling me about this doctor's new approach, using platelet-rich plasma to improve endometrial receptivity that might help me, and I'm not sure what to think as my medical curiosity piques, momentarily overriding my bitter disappointment over the non-kiss.

Lucas's eyes are so dark and intense in the streetlights. "Early results seem promising, especially for women who've had previous implantation failures. I thought...well, you might want to know more about it."

I'm touched by his thoughtfulness, even though

part of me kind of still hopes he'll stop talking and kiss me. I'm so torn right now, I have to keep my head on straight. I don't need a man to kiss me. I need to get pregnant before it's too late. And if he wants to help me, then, great... I guess.

"That's... Thank you, Lucas. I'd definitely be interested in learning more about this."

He smiles, and I can't help a twinge of despair as I see how happy this is making him. He doesn't want to kiss me at all.

"Great. I'll send you Mei-Ling Tan's details," he says, and he lingers a moment, holding his jacket in his arms like a barrier until he nods again and gets into the car.

As he drives away, I'm left with a swirling mix of emotions that I don't really know what to do with. I'm disappointed that he didn't just kiss me, and excited about the potential of a medical breakthrough. And more than a little concerned that my newfound independence is being threatened at every turn by my growing feelings for Lucas Bennett.

CHAPTER TWELVE

I HOLD THE ultrasound wand steady as Rose examines the screen. Denise Caldwell is biting her lip, her eyes flicking between us and the monitor. The room seems to be humming with anxious energy, but it's not all because of our patient, who's returned to see if her new treatment plan is helping.

"There," Rose says, pointing. "You can see the follicle. It's a good size."

Denise's face lights up. "So, I'm ovulating?"

Rose smiles, a warm, reassuring curve of her lips. "It looks very likely."

I wipe the gel from Denise's abdomen and help her sit up. "This means you have a real shot at conceiving naturally, Denise. Keep tracking your cycle and continue with the yoga and Pilates. And the early-morning smoothies?"

She laughs. "Green ones, every day, Doctor."

"Great," I say. "We're very optimistic."

Tears spring to Denise's eyes suddenly. "I am

so beyond grateful. Thank you, both of you. This is just…the best news."

Rose hands Denise a tissue and they chat as my phone pings in my pocket. I know instinctively who it is and I feel my shoulders tense. Mabinty has sent three more messages, each one a little more insistent than the last.

I open the thread and type.

I'm sorry. I can't do this.

I hesitate for a moment, then delete it. Instead, I write:

Let's talk later.

I owe her that, I think. I send it and put the phone in my pocket.

As Denise leaves the room, Rose's shoulders slump ever so slightly. I've noticed she's been more tense than usual, ever since I brought up the trial at her place and she agreed to find out more. Her appointment with Dr. Mei-Ling Tan is today.

"How are you feeling about your call this afternoon?" I ask her.

She pauses, fiddling with a chart, then with her necklace, which tells me she's nervous. "I really appreciate you setting up the call, Lucas."

I nod, but something knots in my stomach.

"You'll be in good hands. Just remember, it's still experimental."

"Every treatment was experimental once." She closes the chart with a snap. "I need to believe in something." Then she sighs and perches heavily against the desk. "Do you really think I have a chance with this?"

I rub the back of my neck, buying time. "It's not that I don't believe in the science, Rose. You know that. It's just... I don't want you to go through any more heartache. You have enough on your plate as it is."

The words fall out of me before I can stop them and I curse my stupid mouth. I just made it very obvious I've been thinking about it. And her. I cross to the window, stare too long and hard at the trees outside. There's vulnerability in her voice when she speaks and it twists my insides.

"Why do you care about this so much, Lucas?"

The question hangs in the air like a live wire. I force my back to stay turned so she can't see my face. This is an invitation. She wants an answer, an acknowledgment that there's something here, maybe? It's pretty hard to ignore how the air buzzes whenever we're alone now. It's another gamble on her part to even be asking me this, but I have to stay strong. This woman is having a baby and it's not going to be with me. Never mind that I've started to imagine a future where she's more than my colleague. Or that I'm terrified that if she fails at this, it will break her, and I can't stand the thought of her broken.

"Rose," I say, choosing my words carefully. "I care because I like to think you're my friend. And because I know what it's like to want something so badly that it consumes you."

Does she know I'm talking about her now? I think of the dinner at her house, how natural she looked holding Lily's babies, how her laughter made me feel more at home than that amazing lasagna. I'm already too involved in this woman's affairs. I should take this whole trial thing as my cue to walk away, to squash this crush once and for all. She'd never cross the line with a colleague after what happened with her husband, and we don't even want the same things.

Rose is still studying me. "Are you okay?"

"Me?" I say, taken aback.

"How are things going with Mabinty? You're meeting up when she's in town, right?"

I frown at her, scratching at my chin. The silence stretches. I'm shocked that Rose even remembers Mabs has that conference in Chicago this week.

"I didn't say I'd see her," I admit.

"Don't you want to get your record player?" she continues, and I feel myself bristle. How does she know about the record player?

"I saw a message pop up on your phone when I was in your car, on the way to my place. She was pretty sure you were meeting up, but you never said anything to me so... Oh, gosh, it's none of my business, is it, if you did or if you didn't?"

She looks at her hands now, embarrassed. So she saw that message and said nothing? I don't know how to take this. I swipe my hand across my head and jaw, also embarrassed.

"Sorry," Rose says now, flustered. "I should go take this Zoom call. Wish me luck."

I am still reeling from her words, but I catch her forearm as she walks past and squeeze it in support. She freezes under my grip. I want to say so many things. I want to show her how Mabinty is my past and not a concern for her at all, but I can't cross any lines here. She's made her decision to get pregnant on her own, and I have offered her this chance with the trial, and now I have to ignore how much I want to spend more time with her *outside* this hospital.

"Good luck," I manage.

I watch her leave the room as the knot in my stomach tightens.

It felt so unexpectedly nice being at her place the other night, playing with the twins, getting all caught up in their games and chaos. I didn't think I could ever feel so at ease in that type of situation, but with her, and Lily and Theo it just felt...natural. I want to believe that everything will work out for Rose on her own, that the science will hold, that her hope will be enough. But

I also know it's a long shot, and there's me, too, now, stuck in the middle of it all. I don't know how to feel about any of this, not about her, not about us and not about the family I've spent so long convincing myself I didn't want.

The rest of the afternoon blurs together: consultations, a quick surgery, more consultations. I catch glimpses of Rose in the hallways, in the staff lounge, always moving, always focused, but I like to think I know her a bit better now. She's a workaholic. So am I. It's one of the reasons we've worked well together since I joined the department. But like me, she works to escape whatever else she's got going on, the things she can't control as easily. Like getting pregnant. I want to ask her how the call went, but she has to come to me. It's not my business.

At five thirty I retreat to my office and close the door. I'm tired, but I still have files to look at. I lean back in my chair and stare at the ceiling, letting my mind wander. It soon wanders back to Rose.

The thing is I've always admired Rose. Even before I met her, I read about her work. She's published, respected. But over the past few weeks, that admiration has shifted gears and all I want to do sometimes is kiss her. Those eyes undo me. I see the woman behind the accolades now, too, the one who tends to a garden to keep her demons at bay, who buys feather boas for her niece, who still flinches at the mention of her ex-husband. I see her, and I care. More than I should.

My phone buzzes on the desk, pulling me from my thoughts. It's a text from Rose.

Can we talk?

My heart does a stupid little lurch.
I type back.

Sure. Where?

Her reply is immediate.

Your office.

I don't have time to wonder what she needs before there's a soft knock at the door. I open it to find her standing there, arms crossed, an unreadable expression on her face that's jarring.

"Come in," I say, stepping aside.

She walks to the center of the room but doesn't sit. I close the door and wait.

"I thought I should let you know how it went," she starts, then stops. "But, Lucas, I don't want to put you in an awkward position."

I fold my arms across my chest so as not to do something silly, like reach for her and tell her it's probably too late for that. "What do you mean?"

She takes a deep breath. "Is it something you even want to know about?"

Is she testing me? I swear she is testing me.

"Rose—" I pause. No. She's a professional. We are at work. She is probably only involving me because I'm the one who initiated her participation in the trial. And if I revoke my interest now it would only seem selfish and cold. "Tell me," I finish.

She studies my face, searching for something. Maybe she finds it, because she nods slowly and some of the tension in her features eases. She tells me how the preliminary data is promising. How so far they've seen significant improvements in endometrial receptivity in a majority of participants.

"I asked about the risks, of course," she continues. "There are risks of infection and complications, but they're minimal. Doctor Tan's biggest concern is the emotional toll. They have to make sure all participants are fully prepared for the possibility that it may not work. I have a psychological examination later this week, and then I guess we will take it from there."

I watch the flicker of doubt and fear cross her face. She feels like this is a last resort, which it shouldn't be, but that's not for me to say.

"Even so, my background makes me an ideal candidate, apparently. He said he'd be thrilled to have me on board."

"That's great, right?" I do my best to sound as happy for her as I should be.

Silence. I can almost hear Rose's thoughts whirring, calculating, weighing. "It is…great," she says after a moment, but I see the conflict blazing in her green eyes. Something beyond my control forces me to reach out a hand again. I press it to hers and she looks at it before letting out a long sigh. For the smallest moment she leans in toward me, as if she wants to rest her head against me. Then she seems to think better of it and steps away quickly, shaking her shoulders like she's shedding a weight.

"This is weird," she says, casting her gaze back to mine.

"It is, a little," I agree, but I don't know if we mean the same thing anymore. This whole situation feels like it's getting out of hand.

I think of Mabinty and the fights we had about children, and about the life we wanted to build before we started taking different paths that only led us further away from each other. Before we grew up and grew apart; not that she'd admit that's what happened. She accused me of being selfish in that hotel room in Dubai, of putting my career above everything else. Maybe she was right. Or maybe I was just scared, like Rose is now.

I've been scared my whole life that my father's emotional neglect when I was a kid might somehow transfer, that I also work too hard to give a kid the attention it would deserve, that I'd regret it, if I brought new life into the world. Rose is scared of a lot worse, but she's doing this, anyway. She is carving out a future for herself that can't involve me. All the more reason to take a big step back.

CHAPTER THIRTEEN

THE PAST SIX weeks have been a blur, thanks to work, the wedding plans and a chaotic whirl of blood tests and treatments involving multiple trips across town to yet another clinic. I can't believe how quickly time has passed since I joined the medical trial. I'm not pregnant yet, but I have more hope than ever before, and I can't stop thinking how I've got Lucas to thank for it. Not that I've had much to do with him lately.

"Everything looks great, Emily," I say, studying the ultrasound as the wand hovers over her swollen abdomen. She's ten weeks in now, and the screen shows a tiny flickering heartbeat. "Your baby's growing right on track. Look at this cute little bean. Your blood pressure is a little high, but we're monitoring that."

Emily's eyes light up and I'm happy that for the first time in a long time, I actually don't feel quite as envious of another woman's success. "I can't believe it. After so many tries, it just feels unreal, Doctor Carter."

I squeeze her hand. "Believe it. This is the home stretch for the first trimester."

"I can believe it. I keep craving red meat. Nathaniel's getting a reputation at the butcher's," she laughs, and I tell her to eat what her body asks her for. We're just discussing the potential merits of indulging in more chocolate bars when the door opens and Lucas walks in. My stomach tightens.

"How are you doing, Mrs. Hanson?" he asks our pregnant patient, flashing a warm smile.

I step back, letting Lucas take a closer look at the screen. "Emily's doing wonderfully. Strong heartbeat, perfect measurements," I announce, while watching his brown eyes crease at the corners. Why does he have to be so handsome?

I watch Lucas as he explains how the hormone support is still crucial, how and why we'll continue the progesterone, how high blood pressure is more common in pregnancies from fertility treatments, noting how my heart does its usual traitorous leap every time he looks my way, or asks me a question.

He's been distant since he told me he cared because he was my friend. I dwelled a lot on that word, the way he said *friend*. I thought there was something more in his eyes and in his tone when he said it, but maybe I was just seeing what I wanted to see. I made myself believe he wanted to kiss me. Then I made myself believe he didn't. Then I forced myself to focus on the trial and my amazing independent self because who needs a man?

If only my heart wouldn't keep calling out for something else.

As Emily leaves, I steal another glance at him. He's already looking ahead, his mind somewhere else. Back with Mabinty, possibly? I guess if he was, it would explain why he's pulled back. I keep telling myself it doesn't matter, that I'm used to being alone, that I should have learned my lesson with David, but his emotional absence stings more than I'd like to admit. I had to give him a chance to tell me if he felt the same, a chance to hear if he also thought there was something between us. But he never wanted anything more than friendship.

"How's the trial going?" he asks suddenly, charging into my thoughts.

I pause, frowning. I can't help a little bitterness seeping into my words. "You haven't asked about it until now."

He rubs the back of his neck. "I didn't want to overstep."

"It's going well," I say, feeling a bit awkward. Then I turn to him, crossing my arms. "I'm feeling pretty good, even if I've missed our conversations lately."

He nods, then shifts his weight on his feet. He waits a while, apparently considering his next words. "How's the wedding planning?"

I shrug. "I found a great pianist."

"Excellent," he says, but he looks almost uncomfortable. Was he expecting me to ask him to play after Lily and Theo almost forced him into it at our house that time? I bite my lip.

"Did you get the invite?" I ask, filling the silence. "All the staff received one."

"I got it. I'll be there," he says. "I can't miss the twins riding down the aisle, throwing those petals."

I can't fight my smile just picturing it. Theo is super excited to put Lucas's suggestion about that into action. A small part of me wishes Lucas and I could go to the wedding together, as each other's date, but that would not look in the least bit professional to the other Evergreen attendees, and of course, neither would he want to. At least I'll see him there. I try to sound casual when I ask, "Will you be bringing a date? Mabinty?"

"No," he says, and there's a finality in his tone that makes me believe him. "We've been over for a long time. I thought you knew that."

I shrug, not wanting to admit that I've been keeping tabs on him. On them. I also can't afford to notice the way he looks at me even more intently, almost questioningly, as he says it. I searched for her on social media. I know all about her fertility app, her awards for various tech accomplishments, but she's surprisingly quiet on the topic of romance. "But you met up with her, right?"

"No," he says, like he's drawing a line under it, and I bite my tongue.

"Sorry, it's none of my business."

"Is that why you keep asking?" he retorts, and I feel the blush creep right up my chest to my face before he studies me so hard I can almost feel his eyes pressing into my cheek.

"No," I say, willing my entire face to stop flaming like a forest fire. "But I'd like it if we could be honest with each other. I was starting to value our…friendship."

Friendship. Oh, why did I have to say that awful word? I need him in the friend zone, though. He's safer there. I'm safer there.

"How's the urban exploring going?" I ask. Anything to lighten the air in here, though I don't miss the smirk on his face, or the way he's picked up a pen and started tapping it absently to his thigh, as if to distract his fingers? I know mine are itching to touch him, to feel like I did when his hand was in mine that one time…that one time I've clung to. I am a crazy person. I need to stop reading into everything he says and does—this is so not me.

He drops the pen with a click of its tip. "A few friends are coming into town for it this weekend. If you're not put off by the last time, you could join us. We're finally going to the Old Prairiewood Asylum."

I hesitate. The last time I went with him on one of these things, it didn't exactly end well with that poor woman ending up in the ER. It was reckless and stupid and…whatever, it was fun. And I've missed his company. "Sure. Why not? I love a good séance."

He looks taken aback for a minute, like he fully expected me not to accept his invitation. He stands up. "Well, I can't promise the séance but…"

"I was joking. I can't think of anything worse. Please, no séance."

He laughs and, oh my, his eyes when he laughs. I'm gone. What am I doing?

"Great. I'll text you the details," he says. Then he looks at me differently, almost apologetically. My heart falls out of step when he says, "For the record, I've missed our friendship, too, Rose."

I bite down hard on my cheeks. The word *friendship* makes me cringe, every single time, no matter which one of us says it. But it's for the best. And if he does only want to be friends, then surely I can at least try to start feeling the same way? I'm going to be a mother soon. I can feel it. So I might as well start having some fun as a single woman…in an asylum?

The door swings open, making me start. We're summoned outside to where our next patient is sitting, patiently waiting. But it's clear we have to see to someone else first. A nurse is on her knees in front of her, taking her details, but I know her.

"Ms. Tallison, what's going on?"

The black-haired woman in her midforties looks up at me. Her face is pale and her hand is gripping her stomach, the other fumbling for something to hold on to.

Lucas is on her in a second, his voice calm but clipped. "We need to examine you, Ms. Tallison. Now."

We both guide her into the exam room and shut the door behind us. She sinks into the soft chair right by the door, as if she can't move any farther. I can see it in her eyes. Panic. Real, raw panic. She's pregnant. She was trying for a year before going with IVF. She was ecstatic to get pregnant and everything seemed to be going to plan. But now something is very wrong.

"The pain," she gasps, her breathing shallow. "It wasn't this bad when I left the house. I mean it was bad, but not this…" She falters as her face scrunches up and my stomach tightens.

"Where's the pain?"

She presses her palm hard into her lower abdomen, wincing. "It's bad, I can't…"

Lucas kneels beside her, hands already moving across her abdomen, assessing. I grab the doppler from the cart and come closer, locking eyes with him for just a second. I know what he's thinking.

"Can you manage?" Lucas says, encouraging her up. His voice is steady but the set of his jaw says everything right now. "We need you to lie down."

The woman nods but hesitates, gripping the chair as if letting go will make the pain worse. I pull over the ultrasound machine. "Take it slow," I tell her, guiding her up along with Lucas, and helping her down to the exam table.

"Breathe with me," I say, setting up the machine. "Deep in through your nose. Hold it. Out through your mouth."

She tries, but the pain hits her again, hard. Her back arches, her hand flying to her stomach, her nails biting into her palms, then into Lucas's arms. Lucas moves quickly, positioning the probe on her abdomen as I adjust the screen. The image comes up, grainy at first, and then—there. The baby. It's early, but it's there. Heartbeat strong. Relief flickers through me, but it's too soon to relax. Her ovaries. That's what we need to see.

I scan lower, biting the inside of my cheek. There. The left ovary. It's swollen, twisted. Ovarian torsion. Damn.

"Lucas." I point at the screen, my voice low. He sees it, too, and his eyes narrow.

"We need to operate," he says, no hesitation. His hands are already pulling off his gloves. "Doctor Carter, can you prep her?"

Ms. Tallison's eyes widen, her breathing speeding up again. "Operate? But—but the baby—"

I step closer, keeping my voice calm but firm. "Your baby's fine. We need to untwist your ovary. It's necessary to protect the pregnancy at this point, and your future fertility. It's a quick procedure, but we need to act now."

Her lip trembles, tears welling up, but she nods, trusting us. She doesn't have a choice.

I call down to the OR, my fingers moving even faster than my thoughts. Lucas is already in motion. He glances at me, giving a quick nod, and for a second I catch a glimpse of something beneath that calm. Worry. We have to move fast.

Lucas makes the first incision. The rest of the room fades out. The ovary is twisted like a rope on itself and her blood flow is severely compromised. Time is running out.

"Clamp here," I say, handing him the instrument. He does, and for a moment I forget about the fact we've barely spoken outside work lately. We're a team; this is why we are here. Nothing else matters. I get into my head way too much when I don't keep busy, always have done. It's why I keep myself on busy mode, always.

He untwists the ovary carefully, too carefully for the amount of time we have, but I don't rush him. We're too close. One wrong move, and she could lose it.

"Blood flow is returning," I say as the color

comes back. It's like watching the life crawl back into a body. We're not out of the woods yet, not at all, but it's a start.

Lucas exhales slowly, his shoulders dropping just a fraction. He looks up at me, and his deep brown eyes are sharp. "Good?"

I nod. "Good."

Lucas closes her up, clean, efficient. By the time he's finished, it's like the whole room exhales with us. The tension breaks. Ms. Tallison is stable now, thank goodness. The baby is safe. We got to her just in time.

Outside the OR, we strip off our gowns. I lean against the wall for a second, trying to let the adrenaline drain out of me, but my heart's still pounding in my ears. Lucas glances at me.

"You all right?"

I nod and turn away, excusing myself from his presence and making for the restroom. I don't quite trust my voice just yet. There's nothing to say, not really. We did our job. That's all that matters.

I scrub at my hands. They're shaking. This will stick with me for a long time, maybe forever; the way she looked at us, the fear in her eyes. Ms. Tallison is divorced. IVF was her last shot. She's older than even me. This is literally her last resort, her only shot at motherhood.

It's not enough just to get pregnant. There are a thousand things around a pregnancy that can go wrong, and if something like this ever happened to me, when I was all alone... Lily would be there. Of course, Lily would be there. And my dad, Geoff, who's always been my rock. Mom's been in Spain for years with her new husband, Miguel, but we talk on the phone. She's here for me when I need her. My family and my friends are all I'd need.

And surely, I would find the strength to try again if something happened like this. I always find the strength to try again, all by myself, because I am strong, and I am independent and I don't need a man.

Why am I still shaking?

I'm lying to myself, that's why.

CHAPTER FOURTEEN

THE SOFT JAZZ drifting from my speakers takes me back to a cramped New York apartment, and Mabinty's perfume lingering in the air with the incense sticks she used to burn to hide the smell of her burnt food. I was always the chef in that relationship. I shake off the memories and silence the music. My coffee has already gone cold in my hands. I pour it down the sink and check the time. I need to get to the asylum soon. I'm meeting everyone there. Rose, too.

I pick out a shirt and sweater, unravel the red scarf from the hanger on the back of the closet door and check my reflection just as my phone buzzes—a text from work about an upcoming fertility case. Work. That's what I should be focusing on, not Rose's questioning emerald eyes, or the way her smile makes my chest tighten every single time.

But as I reach for my jacket, guilt gnaws at me. I never told Rose about meeting Mabinty again. It was innocent enough—just retrieving the old record player—but why did I keep it from her? I outright lied to her, actually. Why?

"Because you're an idiot," I mutter, running a hand across my head. The truth is I don't want Rose to think there's anything left between Mabinty and me. But lying by omission? That's not me. Not usually.

I zip up my jacket hard and face the mirror again. "You're making a mess of this, Lucas."

Rose's face swims before me—hurt and confusion when I pulled away after that almost-kiss outside her place, weeks ago. I was trying to protect her, protect myself. But those walls I've built because of Mabinty, because of my dad? They're crumbling every time she looks at me lately.

I'm halfway to the train when my phone buzzes again. This time, it's Rose.

Hey, just wanted to confirm this place is absolutely perfect for a séance.

My fingers hover over the keys as I smile. Keep it professional, keep it cool, Bennett. But I can't help myself.

Oh, I bet. Did you bring the sage?

I hit Send before I can second-guess myself and hurry on toward the train. I'm a little late, she's already there, probably mingling with the others in the group. Her reply comes as I descend into the subway.

Tons of the stuff. :)

That simple smiley face shouldn't make my heart race, but here we are. I shove the phone into my pocket and board the train.

"You're in trouble, Bennett," I whisper to the empty carriage. "Big trouble."

I spot Rose across what used to be the Old Prairiewood Asylum parking lot, now overgrown with weeds and a few abandoned shopping carts. Her bright red, knee-length coat stands out like a beacon against the looming gray abandoned building. She's wearing it loose over dark jeans, her chestnut hair swept into a messy bun. My heart skips a beat as I approach them. I have unwittingly worn a scarf that matches her coat.

The urban explorers are already chatting with her, and I can't help but smile at how easily she fits in. As I approach, I overhear her discussing the structural integrity of old buildings with one of the group members. I didn't know she knew about things like this, but there's probably a lot I don't know about Rose, including what it's like to kiss her.

"Lucas!" Rose calls out when she sees me, her

green eyes lighting up. "I was starting to think you'd chickened out."

I grin, closing the distance between us. "Never. I love a good ghost hunt."

She grimaces but her eyes are alight with the kind of spirit I haven't seen in a while.

The asylum looming behind us is a hulking mass of crumbling brick and shattered windows. The dreary sky casts an eerie pallor over everything, which seems to match the building's foreboding aura quite fittingly. I was only half joking about the ghosts.

Rose shivers slightly, glancing back at the structure. "This place looks a bit more intense than that theme park we explored last time."

I place a reassuring hand on her shoulder, ignoring the spark of electricity at the contact. "Don't worry. We've got some pretty experienced people here."

She nods. "Including you?"

"Including me," I confirm, but I can see the apprehension in her eyes. Before I can say more, one of the group leaders calls out.

"We've found a safe entrance around back. Let's move!"

As we round the corner, a light drizzle begins to fall from the bleak-looking sky. The group crowds around a partially boarded-up window, discussing the best way in.

"Ladies first?" I offer, extending a hand to Rose.

She raises an eyebrow. "Such a gentleman," she teases, but takes my hand, anyway.

As I help her through the window, I'm acutely aware of her closeness, the warmth of her skin against mine. She stumbles slightly on the other side, and I instinctively reach out to steady her, my hands on her waist.

"Thanks," she breathes, her face inches from mine.

For a moment, we're frozen. My heart speeds like a train on a track as our eyes lock, and for a fleeting second it feels like everyone else disappears and we're back on her driveway.

But just as quickly as it appeared, the moment is broken as one of the other explorers calls out that they've found something interesting. We both step back quickly, our hands falling away from each other. The group gathers around an old medical table covered in rusted tools and empty vials. Rose looks a little green at the sight of it all as I position myself opposite her, but I can tell she's trying to hide it.

"Looks like this was some kind of doctor's office," one of the explorers, a tall guy with shaggy hair, comments.

Rose nods absentmindedly, her eyes scanning the room. "I wonder what kind of experiments they were doing here."

I shrug, still watching her closely. "Probably better off not knowing."

The asylum's interior is exactly what I pictured, a haunting tableau of decay with a musty smell, like various things have suffered and rotted here over time, birds and rats included. Peeling paint hangs from the walls like tattered skin, and rusted gurneys litter the corridors. Our footsteps echo ominously in the cavernous space as we step around them, poking our heads into rooms that are either eerily empty or packed with dilapidated furniture, old linen carts, metal bed frames with broken springs sticking out like weapons. One room is particularly odd. I follow Rose inside as the rest of the group wanders on past us, and she stands in front of a cobweb-covered dresser and closet, standing like hollowed-out skeletons.

"It's freezing in here," Rose whispers, rubbing her arms. Her coat is such a vivid red against the monochromatic room that I feel like we're in a movie as I walk up behind her and shine my flashlight into the drawers, pulling out pieces of old yellowed paper. Bills. "They say the cold spots are where the ghosts hang out."

She shoots me a skeptical look. "Really, Lucas? Ghosts?"

I grin. "I think this was the old reception room, or office," I say, handing her the bills. She studies them in intrigue while I tell her about the building's legends.

"There's the story of the Weeping Nurse, still searching for her lost patients. And the one about the Mad Doctor. His laughter supposedly echoes through the east wing on stormy nights."

As if on cue, thunder rumbles outside, and rain begins to pelt the broken windows. Rose turns on her heel and almost bumps into me as she leads the way back out of the room. I don't miss how she folds the old papers and puts them into her coat pocket. I'm so glad a part of her is enjoying this.

Room after room reveals remnants of a past best forgotten: grime-infested tiling in echoing bathrooms, threadbare mattresses with suspicious stains and down one particularly spooky corridor, iron bars. We peer into the end room, at the bottom of a long corridor, and I can almost see a shudder ripple down Rose's spine as she takes in the scene. I tell her about a haunted cell and she rolls her eyes. "Very atmospheric. Next, you'll tell me—"

A sudden crackling sound startles us both, causing me to bump into a rusty wheelchair in our path. A shower of pebbles crumbles from the cracked ceiling, echoing eerily in the silence. Rose grabs my arm, pointedly avoiding my gaze as she playfully admonishes me. "Watch where you're going, Lucas."

"It's probably a bird," I tell her as she releases me.

"Probably." When she looks back at me from

the window, there's something about those green eyes sparkling under the dim light that makes me completely forget we are standing in an abandoned asylum filled with possibly deranged spirits.

I beckon her into another room attached to this one and we start inspecting a cluster of empty patient beds. Their sheets are all yellowed and stiff with age. A small pile of tattered books sits in a long-abandoned common area at the end. Rose picks up one of them, flipping through its brittle pages with fascination, before placing it gently back on the pile.

Then, another sudden creaking sound from the previous room makes her jump. I shoot her a reassuring smile, though I can feel the hairs on the back of my neck standing up as well. I'm not going to say it out loud, but it really feels like we're not alone, even though the group is still walking around upstairs.

"Let's get out of here," I tell her, and we're almost at the door when she lets out another shriek. This one is a cry of pain.

I'm at her side in an instant, doctor mode kicking in.

"It's just a scratch," she says, clasping her hand and pointing to a rusty spring sticking up from one of the beds. I can see the blood welling up already. It's a bit more than just a scratch. I pull out a small first-aid kit from my pocket.

"Let me take a look."

I clean the cut, kneeling on the dirty floor.

"Always prepared, aren't you, Doctor?" Rose teases.

"Well, I know how trouble follows you, flower girl."

I dab at her wound with antiseptic and hand her a Band-Aid, and her laughter fades to a soft smile as her fingers brush mine. She knows how much I've come to care about her. Even when she does something as simple as graze her hand, everything stops until I've helped her. My heart is thumping wildly against my chest. The uncomplicated act of cleaning up her wound has somehow turned into an intimate exchange, and I am trying so hard to mask the electrifying tension coursing through me.

"I'm glad we're friends again, Lucas," she says.

The word *friends* hits me like a punch to the gut. "Are you sure that's all you want us to be?"

Rose's eyes widen. For a heart-stopping moment, I think I've made a terrible mistake, voicing that question out loud. She looks at me for a brief second more before dropping her gaze to my lips. The unspoken question hangs heavy in the eerie air between us. "You're killing me," I tell her, and she moans softly, closes her eyes, bows her head low.

I gently cup her face, my thumb grazing her soft skin as I tilt her chin up. Her breath catches in her throat, followed by another moan that's dripping with every ounce of the longing I feel, too. Then, I'm not sure who moves first, but I'm kissing her, or she's kissing me. We're kissing, passionately. Her lips are soft and urgent against mine, and I pull her closer, all the weeks of pent-up longing pouring out in this one incredible kiss.

Suddenly, the sound of footsteps echoes nearby. Too close, considering we're alone. We spring apart, breathing heavily.

"Did you hear that?" Rose hisses.

I nod, scanning the empty hallway. "It must be the others," I say, but I'm not convinced.

Another peal of thunder, closer this time, and Rose grabs my hand. We dash through the corridors, half scared, half exhilarated, bursting out into the rain-soaked parking lot. As we stand there getting drenched, Rose starts to laugh. I've never heard her laugh like this. This is something pure, untamed. It's a kind of laughter that starts deep down in the belly and jumps up through the throat to paint the air all kinds of colors I can't even describe. It's contagious, infectious even. Just the sound of it fills my senses until I lose myself in its resonance and I can't help but join in.

"Some urban explorers we are," I tell her, taking off my scarf and wrapping it around her neck.

Rose grins up at me, raindrops clinging to her eyelashes. "We're the worst," she says, and this time, it's definitely she who kisses me first.

CHAPTER FIFTEEN

THE AROMA OF sizzling peppers and cumin wafts through Lucas's apartment. It's so cozy in here, especially with the smell of his Tex-Mex menu mingling with the pitter-patter of rain against the giant windows. I've never really minded the rain in Chicago. After today's events, I love it.

I lean against the sleek kitchen island, watching him expertly flip tortillas on the griddle as part of the meal he casually hinted he'd prepare for me weeks ago. I'm kind of flattered he remembered and offered to cook it tonight, for everyone.

Some of the urban explorers are chatting animatedly in the living area, gathered around on the two couches facing each other. They were planning on going somewhere else for food, but Lucas offered a more homely shelter from the weather. I was planning on going home myself, but after that kiss, and the offer of Tex-Mex, I thought why not, and accepted the invite to his place.

His movements when he cooks are fluid, graceful, confident—just like when he's in the operating room. I can still feel his hot mouth on mine when I close my eyes. I shouldn't have…but I wanted to. It's been a long time since I've been kissed like that.

"Rose, can you grab the salsa from the fridge?" Lucas asks, flashing me a quick smile before grabbing up some avocados.

I nod, and my fingers brush against his as I hand him the cold jar. The simple touch sends a jolt through me, and I'm right back in the asylum, kissing him like a crazy person. I couldn't have stopped if I'd tried.

The apartment is a testament to Lucas's stylish, modern taste—all traditional furnishings, metallic touches, exposed brick walls. The floor-to-ceiling windows make a breathtaking showcase of Chicago's skyline and I love how the city's lights are twinkling at us through the rain-streaked glass. But what caught my eye on the way in was the grand piano in the corner. He's set it up to be the star of the whole apartment. I bet he's an incredible player to have done this. I love the way its ebony surface is gleaming under the soft lighting, almost begging someone to play it. The thought of him playing just for me sends an illicit thrill right through to my bones, but I push it aside. I'm here as a colleague, nothing more. That kiss was a mistake.

I think.

A very sexy, super-hot mistake that I want more than anything to happen again.

I join the urban explorers as they gather around the dining table, their excited chatter filling the room. It's an apartment for hosting, not like our house, which is filled head to toe with toys and old baby stuff, which Lily says she's keeping for me, of course.

"Did you hear those weird noises in the asylum?" Cheryl shudders. "It was like...whispers in the walls or something, so creepy. And footsteps."

Mark, another explorer, shakes his head. "Probably just birds nesting in the rafters. Old buildings are full of them. You hear what you want to hear in these places."

Someone points out that they didn't really want to hear ghosts, and if they did, they would've done the séance. The conversation turns to nothing but white noise when Lucas appears with a steaming platter of fajitas. Our eyes meet, and for another electrifying moment, I'm transported back to that dimly lit room, feeling his lips on mine, his hands...

"Earth to Rose," Sarah says, snapping me out of my reverie. "What do you think? Ghosts or birds?"

I clear my throat, willing my cheeks not to flush. "As a doctor, I'd say there's usually a logical explanation for these things. But who knows?

Maybe some mysteries are meant to stay unsolved."

Lucas smiles thinly and slides into the seat next to mine. I'm acutely aware of his closeness as we dig into the food, and my eyes won't stop stealing glances at him, despite me willing them not to. The way his hands move as he gesticulates, the deep timbre of his laugh—it's all so distracting. I take a sip of my drink, trying to cool the heat rising within me.

After a moment, Sarah leans in, her voice dropping to a conspiratorial whisper. "Speaking of unsolved mysteries, I could've sworn I saw you two sneaking a kiss back at the asylum. What's the story, huh?"

My fork clatters against the plate. Heat rushes to my face, and just like that, I am struggling to maintain my composure.

"I…uh—" I stammer, searching for words. Mercifully, my phone buzzes in my jeans pocket. "Excuse me," I say, practically leaping from my chair. "I need to take this."

I hurry into the hallway, beyond grateful for the reprieve. It's Lily. I answer, trying to steady my breathing. "Hey, Lil."

"Rose! How'd it go at the Old Prairiewood Asylum? Did you summon the dead with your séance?" Lily's voice is bright, teasing.

I lean against the wall, closing my eyes. "No séance, but… I kissed Lucas."

There's a brief silence, then an excited squeal. "What? Oh, my God, Rose! Details, now!"

I can't help but smile at her enthusiasm. "It just happened. In the moment. It was…"

"Amazing? Just average? Not like you imagined? Come on, give me something!"

"It was…intense," I admit, my voice low. "But Lily, it can't happen again. We work together, it's—"

"Oh, stop it," Lily interrupts. "You deserve this, Rose. Don't I keep telling you that? Accept it. It's been ages since—" She pauses abruptly. "Oh, shoot, you're still with him now?"

She sounds worried and I straighten. "Yeah, why?" Then it dawns on me. "Oh, no, Lily, I totally blanked. I'm supposed to be watching the twins tonight. It's date night for you and Theo!"

She pulls a face. I know her so well that I can literally hear it. "That is why I was calling, yes."

Reality crashes back in and I groan, pressing my forehead against the cool wall. "I completely forgot. I'm so sorry, Lily. I'll head home right away."

"Don't you dare rush home," Lily insists. "You always make these sacrifices and you know I appreciate it, but it's not expected of you. I'll ask Mrs. Hernandez next door to put the twins to bed. She's always offering to help."

I hesitate, suddenly torn between responsibility and the unexpected freedom dangling before me like a gold-plated Lucas-scented carrot. "Are you sure? I don't want to upset them. They love my stories."

"Positive. They'll love her stories, too, I'm sure. Have fun, sis. I want all the details later. He's so very sexy, imagine what those hands could…"

"I'll be back in the morning for the grocery shop," I say quickly, then I cut her off, sucking in a deep breath as guilt and excitement bubble in my chest. It's been so long since I've been in a man's apartment, I almost don't know what I'm supposed to do next, but when I walk back in, the coffee is being served and they're still swapping stories and theories about the asylum.

Lucas catches my eye, raising an eyebrow in silent question. I give him a small nod, feeling a flush creep up my neck, and it only gets hotter when he rests a hand on my knee under the table, like he's claiming me. I like it.

Hours pass in a blur of laughter and animated discussions. As the night wears on, the light fades, the rain continues to pound at the glass and I really feel like I've made new friends, despite having to dodge a few difficult questions from Sarah about the kiss she saw outside.

When the group begins to gather their things, I linger, pretending to be fascinated by the Chicago skyline, visible through Lucas's floor-to-ceiling windows, and his vintage record player. My heart races as I hear the last goodbyes at the door, followed by the soft click of it closing.

Lucas's footsteps approach, and I can feel the tension crackling between us instantly. Neither of us speaks for a moment. The silence hangs heavy as the raindrops patter with what feels like a million possibilities.

"So," he says finally, his voice low.

"So," I repeat.

He smiles. "I didn't expect you to stay."

I turn to face him, acutely aware of how close he's standing. "I didn't expect to, either."

His eyes search mine, and I feel the last shreds of my resolve wavering.

"Rose, about earlier—"

"We probably shouldn't talk about it," I interrupt.

Lucas takes a step closer, and I instinctively back up, feeling the cool glass of the window against my shoulders through my shirt. "Maybe we should," he murmurs.

The air between us feels electric now, fully charged with a new kind of energy. I know I should leave. I should tell him it's time to get the train, time to remember my professional boundaries and what happened last time I launched into something with a colleague, but I can't bring myself to move.

"Rose," he whispers, his voice barely audible. "I meant it when I said you are killing me."

He reaches out, his fingers ghosting along my jawline. As his lips meet mine, all thoughts of propriety and professionalism vanish. In this moment, I'm not Dr. Rose Carter, divorcée, dedicated endocrinologist, responsible aunt. I'm just Rose, a woman on fire, who is allowing herself to feel and to want for the first time in far too long. This time the kiss is three times more passionate than before and I melt into Lucas, my hands tangling in his shirt as I lose myself in the moment, the heat radiating off him only fueling my desire for him. Body to body, skin on skin.

In this moment, there are no thoughts of consequences or regrets. It's just me and Lucas, and I feel like I float through every touch and every kiss, relishing it so I can dredge it back up from my memories later. Somehow, after he presses me gently to the piano keys with a noisy clunk, we end up on the piano stool and he grins against my mouth.

"Are we going too fast? I'll get us a nightcap?" He half stands, still leaning over me, and kisses me again before groaning and tearing himself away. I catch my breath, my fingers brushing the polished surface of the piano for want of something else to do with my hands now that he's clattering around in the kitchen.

The keys are cool beneath my fingertips as I plunk out a simple melody, one I learned as a child. It's been years since I've played, but muscle memory takes over. It's far from being good. I hear Lucas's footsteps behind me, followed by the clink of glass against glass.

"Your drink, my lady," he says, his voice low and intimate in the now quiet apartment.

I nod, accepting the tumbler of amber liquid he hands over. It looks like it's going to burn, but so what. Tonight I'm feeling reckless. "Thanks."

Lucas slides onto the bench next to me, our thighs touching. The warmth of his body, just one limb of it against mine, is intoxicating. "I didn't know you played," he teases.

"Very funny," I reply. "Want to show me how it's really done?"

"If you insist."

I move aside, and after he sips his drink, his long, slender fingers replace mine on the keys. Suddenly, the room is filled with a hauntingly beautiful melody. I recognize it immediately—"Clair de Lune" by Debussy. The music swells and ebbs, Lucas's hands moving with graceful ease, like he's completely at one with the music. Hypnotic. Like his kisses. At one point, he even closes his eyes. I realize I'm watching him in awe and wonder.

"That's incredible," I breathe when the final notes fade away. "Where did you learn to play like that?"

Lucas's eyes meet mine. I spot a hint of vulnerability in their deep brown depths. "My mom insisted on lessons. She said a true gentleman should be able to play at least one instrument. My father played, too. He was pretty good."

"So why did you need lessons? Why didn't your father teach you?"

Lucas shrugs. "He didn't have time. That man was always too busy for me, remember?"

I stare at him, surprised by the sudden bitterness in his tone. He studies the keys, too thoughtfully as he continues. "And the worst part? I've become just like him, haven't I? All work, no real life outside the hospital."

"What about breaking into abandoned buildings and playing piano?" I say. I want to add "what about me?" but I think it's too soon. "You seem to have a lot more going on than you give yourself credit for," I say instead.

"I guess I find room for the things I want," he replies.

I swallow hard. "And what do you want most?"

"I don't know. That's why I work so much. I never really considered anything else other than Mabinty, and the prospect of having her kids, and now I'm…not with Mabs, and I'm definitely not having kids so…"

"She was right," I murmur, suddenly aware of how close we are, and how deep this conversation is getting. I also don't want to hear how opposed to having a family he clearly is right now. "Your mother, I mean. You are a true gentleman."

His hand reaches up, tucking a strand of hair behind my ear. "Rose," he whispers, and then his lips are on mine again. The kiss is different from our earlier ones—slower, deeper, filled with an intensity that makes my head spin. This is too much.

"I should go," I say breathlessly, standing up quickly. The few sips of drink I just had are already going to my head.

I quickly grab my bag and head toward the door. But before I can open it, Lucas's hand reaches out to stop me. He turns me around and kisses me again, softer this time but still full of longing.

"Good night," he whispers against my lips.

"Good night," I reply, but in seconds, his hands are roaming over my body again, igniting a burning inferno inside me that would take diving into the freezing cold river to extinguish. I press myself closer to him, desperate for more contact. Our bodies move in sync. It feels like we've been doing this dance for years, and his fingers intertwine with mine as we move away from the door and into his bedroom. Inside, his hands find my waist, pulling me close.

As we fall onto the bed, I can't help but think how different this feels from anything I've experienced before. Even with David, my ex-husband, it was never like this. Lucas touches me with a reverence that makes me feel wanted in a way I've never known.

"Is this okay?" he asks, his voice husky as he hovers above me. I'm tearing at his shirt now, desperate for more of him.

I nod, unable to find words, letting my fingers do the talking. "More than okay."

What follows is a passionate exploration of each other's bodies that blows my mind with its intensity. Lucas is attentive, responsive to every gasp and shiver. His knowledge of the female anatomy seems to translate into an intimate understanding of my body that literally leaves me breathless and gasping and clutching at the sheets like a wild woman. I'm so in awe of him, but somehow my body knows just how to respond, just how to pleasure him, too. By the time he slides on the condom I am too worked up to do anything but kiss him, and when we move together, it's pretty evident our connection goes way beyond the physical. It's as if Lucas sees me—truly sees me—in a way no one else has before. The intensity of it all is so overwhelming I find I'm blinking back tears—oh, my goodness! Embarrassed, I swipe them away and he asks me if I'm all right, if I want to stop, and I cup his face in my hands, smiling through my tears. "I'm perfect," I assure him. "Don't stop."

The night stretches on in a magical blur of passion and tenderness and whispered words and a million emotions I didn't think I was capable of processing. The way he looks at me and caresses me, it's like he truly appreciates everything about me, every curve, every line, every freckle, and I hope I prove how much I appreciate him, too. When we finally collapse, spent and more than satisfied, Lucas pulls me close, his arm draped protectively over my waist.

"Stay," he murmurs into my hair, already half-asleep. There was never any question that I wouldn't, once we got naked. Besides, the last train left hours ago.

I nestle closer, under his arm. I'll remember this forever, I think, as I allow myself to drift off in his embrace, and when I wake, I blink in shock at the sunlight streaming through the window, before remembering where I am and what just happened.

I take a moment to breathe, to watch this beautiful man beside me, still sleeping peacefully, his breathing deep and even. Carefully, I extricate myself from his hold, trying not to wake him. A clock on the wall shows it's late, gone 10:00 a.m., which isn't surprising, considering we spent most of the night awake, but it's Sunday and I need to get back home. I have chores to do, I promised Lily. I drop a kiss on his lips and tell him to stay where he is, and he mumbles something about making me coffee, then promptly falls back to sleep. I can only smile. He doesn't need caffeine and neither do I; we both need more sleep, but I can't ignore my responsibilities any longer.

As I gather my clothes, my gaze falls on a shelf in the corner. The gifted buckle from the Texan ranch is a humorous feature piece that makes me smile. Records are stacked neatly across several shelves, their spines showing multiple genres, mostly jazz. Something jigs in my mind. The vintage record player in the lounge.

Keeping my footsteps at bare minimum volume, I creep back into the lounge and pad over to it, rubbing my eyes. Sure enough, it's there; I wasn't imagining it. I saw it last night of course, but it barely registered. My mind was all caught up on Lucas.

I rub my arms, the questions and disappointment mounting as fast as the thrill of the evening fades and fizzles out. Isn't this what Mabinty was going to return to him? And didn't he specifically tell me he didn't meet up with her to retrieve it?

He lied.

CHAPTER SIXTEEN

I watch as Rose's fingers glide over the ultrasound wand, the cool gel catching the light as it spreads across Mrs. Chen's abdomen. Her green eyes never leave the screen as she studies the grainy black-and-white image flickering to life.

Mrs. Chen is lying tense on the exam table, gripping the edge of her gown with pale knuckles. Her eyes dart nervously between us, trying to read something—anything—from our expressions. Rose clears her throat softly, her voice laced with the kind of compassion she hasn't extended to me for a week now, not since she snuck out of my apartment that morning.

"Mrs. Chen, I'm seeing multiple small cysts on both of your ovaries. This pattern is consistent with a condition called polycystic ovary syndrome, or PCOS." She glances briefly at me before turning back to the screen, and Mrs. Chen's breath hitches.

"So that... Is that why I haven't been able to get pregnant?"

Her voice trembles with the strain of months—maybe years—of trying and hoping and sitting in rooms like this with strangers probing and prodding her. It's nothing we haven't been through before, but knowing what Rose is going through, or *was* going through with the trial and the sperm donor, makes it hit home harder for me now, too. Not that I know where Rose is at with it all lately, because she doesn't appear to be talking to me.

I step closer, choosing my words carefully. "PCOS can make it harder to conceive, yes, but it's not impossible. The cysts can affect regular ovulation, but there are treatments that can help."

Mrs. Chen presses a hand to her chest, visibly absorbing the information. "So…there's still hope?"

Rose softens, tells her there is definitely hope, which surprises me. Usually, she leaves that part up to me, while she takes on more of a practical approach. Is she phasing me out in any way possible now, because I'm a colleague and she's slept with me, and now she's terrified people will know and start talking, like they did about her and her ex?

As we discuss treatment options, I want to kick a foot through this invisible barrier that Rose has pushed up between us. The first few days admittedly I treated it like a game, something fun we were sharing, me the cat, her the mouse. Only, she hasn't let me catch her yet. Ever since that night, my mind keeps flashing back to the warmth of her soft skin, all her curves and lines, the way she let down her guard, just for a moment, just for me. And now she's acting like nothing happened.

I push the thought aside, forcing myself back into the present.

Mrs. Chen's voice interrupts my wandering thoughts. "What about IVF?"

I nod, folding my arms as I lean against the counter, choosing a reassuring tone to tell her we'll start with less invasive approaches, lifestyle changes and medication, and Rose wipes off the ultrasound wand as Mrs. Chen processes the information, her hands finally relaxing their grip on her gown.

We wrap up the appointment, scheduling Mrs. Chen's follow-up. As she walks out, her shoulders seem lighter, but Rose is more tense than ever. She keeps her eyes on the paperwork, her voice cool, efficient. Cold, even. "We should probably go over her file in more detail later. I'll send you the updated report."

The ache in my chest tightens. "Sure," I murmur, but she's already halfway out the door. I can't take it anymore. I catch her arm gently, my frustration finally boiling over.

"Rose. We need to talk. What's going on? Do you...do you really regret what happened between us so much that you're making out like it didn't happen? I feel like one of those ghosts in the asylum here!"

Her green eyes finally meet mine. I watch a storm of emotions swirling in their depths and for the briefest of moments I think she might open up, but then her walls slam right back into place.

"Doctor Bennett, this isn't the time or place for personal discussions," she says, her tone clipped. "We have patients waiting."

As she pulls away and strides down the hall, I feel like I've been punched in the gut. What the hell happened to the woman I made love to that night? Did I dream it? I thought we connected on a deeper level, deeper than I ever connected with Mabs, now that I think about it. I thought she felt the same, but now it feels like we're back to square one—or worse.

I run a hand across my chin. This is so frustrating. I want to be mad but I'm just…well, I'm pretty hurt, actually. I'm not sure where we stand at all now, or how to fix this. All I can do is wait, I guess.

I straighten my lab coat and head to my next appointment. The day stretches on, full of patients who need my focus and expertise. But even as I immerse myself in my work, it doesn't help like it usually does. I need to know what happened.

I catch her again in the parking lot, and she pulls her red coat tight around her when I call for her, ask her again if we can talk. I must be coming off as a crazy person, but this is what she's done to me. Rose just sighs. Her green eyes scan mine for a moment before she steels herself.

"Lucas, look, it was…lovely. But I don't do emotional connections, especially not with colleagues."

Her words sting, but I push past the hurt. "Rose, I'm not your ex. I'm not David," I tell her, stepping closer. "I know we work together, but I'm not going to hurt you or make things awkward. What happened? Don't you trust me?"

She shakes her head and almost laughs, which irks me more than I let on. "What's so funny?"

She shakes her head again, tightening her jaw, and buries her chin in the collar of her coat. "I don't want anything from you, Lucas. The trial has been successful. I thank you for setting that up for me. I'm doing very well on it, so they say. There's a high chance that a sperm donor insemination will take this time."

I look at her, stunned. "You had the procedure again?" For some reason, the thought of it makes me slightly nauseated.

"Yes, I did."

"Wow, that's…um…" I swallow the stab of disappointment as it hits me, watch the leaves swirling round us in a sudden breeze. "Why didn't you tell me?" I ask her. I can't hide the disillusion in my voice and I hate it.

She lowers her head. "I didn't think you'd want to know," she says, and I press my hands to my head, stepping back from her. "And I was right, judging by your reaction."

"I'm just surprised you did it, after we…"

"After we what, slept together?" She sounds incredulous now. "You don't want anything else from me, Lucas, that was one night of fun and you know it."

I stare at her, completely thrown. "Yes, it was one night of fun, but I was thinking it might turn into a few more nights of fun, and maybe something else," I admit.

Rose stares at me open-mouthed, and I turn and pace away. I can't look at her anymore, knowing what she's done. This situation is pressing all my buttons about kids and families. I don't know what I want but I know what I *don't* want. I don't want to keep living in a world where Rose is being so cold and distant with me. I want *her* in my life. I know that now. I want us to at least try to see if we can be something, and to see if we can navigate what we do and don't want together.

When I look at her again, she has her arms crossed, leaning against the wall. I swear she is blinking back tears. "But… Lucas, you lied to me. You met up with Mabinty when you said you didn't."

I stare at her now, racking my brain, and she rolls her eyes like I'm an idiot, pushes herself off the wall. "The record player? The records? I saw them in your apartment. I can't start anything with a liar, Lucas, especially not one I work with, and who doesn't even want kids."

I'm still staring. So *that's* what this is about? A record player?

"You want me, but you don't want a family. And you're also a liar."

"I'm not a liar, Rose. Why are you so intent on building this case against me?"

"Just forget about it," she clips, swiping at her eyes and straightening her back. "You don't have to explain yourself. You were together a long time."

"Yes, we were," I agree with her. "And no, I shouldn't have to explain myself! You should just trust me."

"I don't," she says, her voice wobbling now. "I don't trust you. I want to, but how can I?"

I don't know what to say to that. This is her issue to deal with, a result of that stupid man she married. What can I do?

Huffing a sigh, she turns around again and makes for her car. I almost follow her but I stop myself. How can I make her understand when she's already made up her mind about me, and us, and the fact that she's now probably expecting a baby ASAP with a random dude she's never met? Now I'm not hurt, I'm mad, actually. What is up with these changing emotions? What is this woman doing to me? When she pulls away from the suddenly too quiet parking lot, I can't help but feel like I've just lost something I never really had in the first place.

The days blur into another week, a monotonous cycle of patients and paperwork. Chicago seems bigger than it ever did, a giant, cold, vast city where Rose and I coexist but barely interact, much like Evergreen General. I catch glimpses of her in the hallways, her brown hair swaying as she rushes past, always with a purpose. In joint appointments, she's efficient and polite, but never personal. A workaholic, like she said she was.

In meetings, we maintain a facade of professionalism. "Doctor Carter, your thoughts on this case?"

"The patient's hormone levels suggest we should adjust the treatment plan." She talks to me, but her eyes never meet mine. I try to ignore the persistent memory of the feel of her skin against mine. The way our bodies spoke to each other, how we guided each other, how damn good it felt inside her, body and mind. Now there's only silence. And she might even be pregnant!

One evening, still trying to get her out of my stubborn brain, I stash the record player in the closet where it can't torture me. I shouldn't have lied about meeting Mabinty, I think, as I shove it behind the rail of coats and jackets. It was the smallest white lie to me, a nonissue, something I said for Rose's benefit...kind of... I've known Mabs practically my whole life. It's not as easy as you might think, cutting ties completely. Besides, I wanted my damn record player!

But understandably, it's huge to her. Rose has been broken and lied to, and kept in the dark, and she thought I was different. She'll probably never trust me again.

In the kitchen, my gaze falls on the wedding invitation stuck to my refrigerator. Lily and Theo's names are embossed in elegant script and I trace the edges of the card. Her sister's upcoming nuptials. The wedding is this weekend already; how time flies. Everyone from Evergreen will be there. I rip the card out from under its magnet and toss it into the trash. The thought of seeing Rose all radiant as I know she will be in her bridesmaid's dress, laughing with others while barely acknowledging me, is too much to bear. I'd crack, or say something, or both, and that wouldn't be fair to anyone.

I reach for my phone. I'm sorry, Rose, I type, but please tell Lily and Theo I won't be able to attend the wedding. I hit Send before I can change my mind.

CHAPTER SEVENTEEN

My phone buzzes over the soft rustle of tissue paper filling the living room as I carefully finish wrapping another faux flower stem. Lily's working alongside me, tucking each silk blossom into its designated glass bottle for the homemade table decorations, and she looks up when I put the device back on the floor a little too hard. My stomach just plummeted through the carpet.

"Lucas can't make it to the wedding," I announce.

Lily's hands pause midwrap. "Oh, Rose. That's a shame."

I force a shrug, trying to ignore the sharp pangs of disappointment tearing through me. I know we haven't exactly been seeing eye to eye but a part of me still expected him to be there on Saturday, with the team. I don't know why.

"It doesn't matter," I say, unconvincingly. "He lied to me about meeting Mabinty. I can't trust someone who does that. It's better off this way."

Lily eyes me sideways. She hands me another

flower to wrap. "Not all men are like David," she says gently. "Did you ever think maybe Lucas only lied because he likes you and was afraid of scaring you off?"

I snort, focusing intently on the delicate petals between my fingers. "Right. Because deception is such a great foundation for a relationship."

"Oh, so you want a relationship with him, do you?" She quirks an eyebrow and smirks, and I wave her off by flapping a flower in her face. "You're being too hard on him," she continues, instantly stirring up the whirlwind of conflicting emotions that's been dormant in my belly since she took my mind off him with this wedding stuff, for all of an hour, probably less.

Part of me wants to believe that Lucas lied because he didn't want to scare me off, but David's trail of lies that ultimately led to me discovering his betrayal left me so scarred, is it any surprise that Lucas's lie was a trigger? I have to trust when to remove myself from situations that are bad for me. I tell Lily so and she sighs. "I just want you to be happy."

I manage a small smile. "I know. And I am, in my own way. I have my work, I have you... That's enough, isn't it? And I have a good feeling this time. I'll get pregnant. It's going to take. I can feel it."

"That's wonderful," Lily says, but her brow

furrows slightly. "But are you sure you're ready to close the door on other possibilities?"

I nod, forcing my mind back to the sterile room at the fertility clinic just the other day: the cold stirrups, the awful, unromantic clinical process, the total opposite to how I felt that night with Lucas in his bed, and in his arms. Maybe that's why, despite my best efforts, I couldn't stop thinking about Lucas the whole time the event was happening. His warm brown eyes, his gentle hands, the way he always seems to know exactly what to say to put patients at ease, the way he knew exactly what to say and do to *me* that night.

"I…" I start, then falter. I have to come clean with my twin at least. "The truth is, Lils—and I know this is terrible—I couldn't stop thinking about him. About Lucas. Even as she was performing the procedure, part of me was wishing… well…"

Lily's eyes widen, then soften. "Oh, Rose."

"I know, I know," I say quickly. "It's ridiculous. Maybe you're right. I've been pushing him away because I'm scared of how much I like him. I am terrified of getting hurt again. Our futures don't align. He doesn't want children, and I… I'm choosing motherhood."

"Maybe you're not giving him enough credit," Lily suggests gently. "People can change their minds, especially when they meet the right person."

I shake my head firmly. I said pretty much this exact thing to him once, and he seemed to contemplate it, but he hasn't said anything to make me think he wants kids, since. "No. I can't build a life on maybes. I already made up my mind."

"I understand," Lily says, although I can tell she's not convinced at all. She knows me, and I can read her face. "But why don't you just ask him to the wedding yourself? Give him a chance to explain, at least."

"Absolutely not," I say, more sharply than I intend. "He's made his decision. He won't be at the wedding, and I'm not going to give him any other signals that I want him there. That's final."

Lily raises her hands in surrender. "Okay, fine, have it your way. I just hate to see you close yourself off like this. You don't have to always be so independent, you know."

"I appreciate your concern, Lil. I do. But this is what's best for me right now."

I grab for another flower and wrap it so tightly that it breaks. I let myself fall back on the carpet, blinking at the ceiling while she offers to pour me a glass of wine. I refuse, obviously. I could be pregnant already. But I can't help wondering if I'm truly convincing Lily I don't want Lucas around, or totally failing to convince myself.

The alarm blares through the clinic. My heart lurches. The emergency code rarely goes off in the fertility department, and my thoughts go to Emily Hanson. Please, not her. She's here now, with Lucas, I think? I move fast down the hall into Room 3B. It's not Emily I find.

Annika Ackerman is curled up on the bed, her face twisted in pain. She's thirty-four, three months pregnant via IVF, and alone. No partner today. No support. Her skin is ashen, and she's gripping her stomach with one hand, the other clawing at the sheets. Lucas is already with her.

"Tell me," I say, moving to his side.

"I—I can't breathe," Annika gasps, her words ragged. "My chest—something's wrong."

I glance at Lucas as he fiddles with an IV. This isn't right.

"She was short of breath and having hot flashes while waiting, but the chest pain hit as soon as she got up to follow me," Lucas says.

My stomach twists. "What's her status now?"

"Vitals are all over the place. Blood pressure's crashing, heart rate's spiking."

He radios down to ER. "We might need backup up here. Possible thromboembolism."

I check the IV, my own voice tightening. "Pulmonary embolism? A clot?"

"One of the risks post-stimulation, even though we hardly ever see it."

Lucas is listening to the radio. "They're sending people up now."

Annika's gaze locks on to mine, her eyes wide

with panic. "I—I can't—" She can hardly speak and her body is trembling. We need to stabilize her now, or this could get worse before anyone's even made it up the elevator. I think of Theo downstairs and pray he's on shift. My hands work before my mind catches up. If the clot moves and blocks anything vital she could go into cardiac arrest.

Annika lets out a low, pained groan. Her hand grips my wrist, cold, shaky. "Am I dying?" she whispers, and it makes my chest constrict.

"No," I say firmly, and Lucas echoes me, though a ripple of fear travels up my spine. "No, you're not dying. You're going to be fine."

The room feels smaller, the air heavier. I can hear Lucas barking orders, but it's all background noise now. We've barely spoken and now we're literally fighting for someone's life together. It puts everything into perspective, really, all the silly grudges we hold on to, all the things we leave unsaid.

It feels like a lifetime before Theo rushes in with the heparin and administers it swiftly. Annika's body responds with a series of jerks, and for a horrifying second I think we might be losing her. "Breathe in. Focus on me," I tell her.

She locks eyes with me, but there's a glassiness there. She's fighting it, but she's fading fast. I swallow. I can't do anything now; it's out of my remit. Theo barks more orders at the guys he came in with and Lucas puts a steady hand to my arm. I lean into him, needing his calmness. These situations rattle me more than they should, knowing I could be pregnant. I won't know for sure, not for a couple of weeks yet, but I might be.

They're pushing more oxygen now, trying to stabilize her as her body fights the clot. Annika's breathing is still ragged, but she's holding on. My voice cracks and I have to leave the room. Lucas follows me, and I turn into him. "We can't lose her, not like this," I tell him, and he puts his hands to my shoulders, steadying me.

"We won't." He knows this is a close one but I can see he's not going to give up, and neither should I. Back in the room the seconds morph into an eternity as the team works tirelessly to save her. The frantic pace of it all finally slows as Annika's vitals begin to stabilize. A little of the suffocating fear recedes from my bones and Theo nods at Lucas, recognition of a job well-done.

Theo presses a hand to my shoulder briefly as they wheel her out, down to the ICU where she'll receive round-the-clock care, and where I will be sure to check on her shortly. As the double doors swing shut behind them, it's just Lucas and me left standing in the emptied room. His gaze sweeps over my face before landing on my trembling hands, still clenched tightly around my lab coat.

"She's in the best hands," he tells me.

"I know." I let out a long sigh. "I thought she might be Emily."

He looks at me in surprise, gently tells me Emily's appointment is next, and I know he knows I'm applying worst-case scenarios to every single one of our pregnant patients. He knows me, and he knows why. I meet his eyes. I want to tell him I'm done with acting like I don't want him around, that Lily was right. I've been pushing him away because I like him so very much, more than I want to, but the words stick in my throat. What if I'm pregnant? He'll want nothing to do with me then, so why would I walk willingly into another disappointment?

I'm saved anyway by my phone, but it's a message from the pianist. My stomach drops as I read it, and I rest my head back against the wall with a sigh.

Now? Really?

"Damn," I mutter. "Of course this would happen now, when my nerves are already shot."

Lucas throws me a questioning look and I shake my head. "The piano player for the wedding. He broke his arm, falling off a ladder. The wedding's tomorrow. I need to make some calls."

I excuse myself, making my way to the cafeteria. I get a coffee, and fresh adrenaline takes over as my fingers fly over the phone screen, reaching out to every musician I know within a fifty-mile radius. No luck. Panic starts to set in. I thought I had everything under control, but I don't. I need to pull it together.

When I return to the exam room, Lucas is finishing up with Emily Hanson's latest exam. I tell her hi, and Lucas looks at me over his glasses. "Any luck?"

I shake my head, defeated. "Nothing. I'm out of options."

Emily looks between us, her hand on her belly. I explain what has happened. Over the recent weeks, Emily has come to know about Lily's wedding, and I've actually come to consider her as more of a friend. I'm excited to meet her and Nathaniel's baby soon.

There's a moment of silence as the three of us think. Then, hesitantly, Lucas speaks up. "I... I could do it. If you want."

I blink, surprised. "What? I thought you couldn't come. You RSVP'd no."

I realize Emily is still looking, but at this point, I don't even care. He told me flat out that he wasn't coming to the wedding, and I haven't questioned him on that decision since, despite wanting to. But now, not only is he changing his mind about attending, he also wants to replace the pianist. I look at him, considering it. Right now he's my only option.

"Are you sure?" I ask him.

"Absolutely," he says, his dark eyes meeting mine. "I um...maybe I was too quick with that

RSVP, huh?" He looks at Emily, who suppresses a giggle, then back to me. "Anyway, look at what Theo—Doctor Montgomery—just did for me… for us," he says.

Us.

He said there could have been an us, and again I pushed him away. Too scared that he'd change his mind for one reason or another. But he's not David.

I take a deep breath. "Okay. Thank you, Doctor Bennett. Really."

As Emily leaves, wishing us both luck, Lucas lingers. "Rose, about Mabinty… I'm sorry. I should have been up-front with you. I promise, no more white lies."

My heart clenches. I want to tell him it's okay, that I forgive him because I kind of have a feeling I know why he did it, but that would open up a whole other can of worms. What if I'm pregnant already? I can't afford to let this friendship slip into anything other than purely platonic territory, not this time.

"Maybe I overreacted," I tell him instead. "I'll see you tomorrow. Thank you again."

Without another look at him, I leave the room, then the hospital. I guess the next time I see Lucas, it'll be at the wedding. I'll just have to be okay with it. But at some point on the drive home, it strikes me that when Emily looked like she knew something was going on with me and

Lucas, I didn't even worry. I wasn't the least bit concerned what people would think. There are bigger issues in a hospital and Lucas *isn't* David. He's proven that already. And all of this is why it's going to be a thousand times harder letting him go.

CHAPTER EIGHTEEN

I CAN'T TAKE my eyes off her. The soft curves of her shoulders, the way her chestnut hair is cascading down her back—she's breathtaking in that dress. A magnificent honor. As if sensing my gaze, Rose turns and our eyes lock. The Botanic Garden takes on an ethereal quality as I step onto the cobblestone path and start toward her across the courtyard.

Fairy lights are twinkling in the trees over the throngs of people milling around the tall reception tables, all looking suave in suits and gowns, sipping from flutes of champagne. Her lavender dress catches the light in all the right places, highlighting her incredible figure as she chats with a man I assume is her father, Geoff. I've heard her mention him a few times. And her mother is here, too. She looks just like Lily and Rose, and she's here with a man. Her second husband, Miguel, I think. I've heard Rose mention her, too. A jolt of longing courses through me as she finally excuses herself and makes her way over, her heels clicking against the stone. I straighten my tie, suddenly aware of every move I make.

"Lucas." Her tone is warm but guarded, just as I expected. "Thanks for coming. And thank you again for agreeing to play piano for the ceremony."

"Of course," I reply as her green eyes dart around, searching. Then I lower my voice. "Rose, please don't act like I'm a stranger."

"Did you come alone?" she asks, ignoring my plea but still failing to sound casual.

"Yes, just me, just like I said," I say, accepting a flute of fizzing liquid as the waiter passes us.

"Well, I'm glad you're here. Lily will be thrilled."

"How is she doing?" I ask in an effort to keep the conversation going. I wish I didn't still want her. She's already made it pretty clear that our one night together was as far as things will ever go, that her priority is motherhood, not a relationship. And I know I don't want any part of that. So why can't I get her out of my head?

"Nervous, excited. You know Lily," she replies, still looking around her. I frown. It's like she doesn't even want to be seen with me. "I should actually go check on her. But I'll see you up there?"

"Absolutely. I'll be at the altar."

She looks up sharply and I shrug. "At the piano?"

Rose's smile doesn't quite reach her eyes as

she tells me she'll see me later. I watch her make her way back through the crowd, leaving her perfume lingering behind. This is every bit as awkward as I thought it would be. What am I even doing here? I feel like I owe it to Theo, though, and Lily, too. I've been practicing the songs nonstop in my apartment, over and over, losing myself in the music, thinking about Rose, of course.

When it's time for the ceremony, I settle onto the piano stool, my fingers poised over the keys. I let the lilting melody of Pachelbel's Canon fill the air as Lily appears at the end of the aisle. She's a vision in ivory lace, her dress hugging her curves, flaring out into a dramatic train on the red-carpeted aisle. I play on while all eyes stay glued to her, and damn if I can't stop seeing Rose in her place. The perfect bride. They're not identical, but they look pretty damn similar from here.

Cameras snap, and more fairy lights set a storybook scene around the ivy-clad pillars and white silk-draped chairs. Tears glisten in Lily's eyes as she takes her first steps toward Theo, waiting in his tailored gray suit at the altar. They really are the perfect couple, everyone agrees. But even as the twins appear in their little wheely cars, throwing petals out behind them, and my fingers keep on with the melody, my gaze keeps drifting to Rose, following her sister. Our eyes lock again and for a moment, it's like we're the only two people in the room. I fumble a chord, my fingers suddenly clumsy on the keys.

Rose's lips quirk into a small smile, and I feel a flush of heat rush to my face. I force myself to focus on the music, on Lily's evident, radiant happiness as she meets Theo at the altar and takes her stance opposite him. But my traitorous eyes keep finding Rose.

As the officiant begins to speak, my mind wanders over long conversations with Mabinty about our own wedding. The arguments about venues, guest lists, even the damn napkin colors. It all seems so trivial at this moment, but now I can see beyond those trivialities. I think we both secretly knew it would never happen. I think she knew it, too. We were both dancing around the inevitable for far too long.

"Do you, Theo Matthew Montgomery, take Lily Anna Carter to be your lawfully wedded wife?"

I wonder if Mabinty's found someone new. The thought doesn't sting like I expected it to. Instead, I feel...nothing. The realization is quite liberating. I hope she finds happiness.

"I do," Theo's voice replies, clear and confident.

I transition into a softer piece as Lily and Theo exchange rings, and the twins giggle, rallying around them. Rose catches my eye again and this time, I don't look away. There's a warmth in her gaze now that draws me in, a different look, almost…regretful.

"You may now kiss the bride."

I play the final chords as Lily and Theo share their first kiss as husband and wife. The applause drowns out the music, but I can't tear my eyes away from Rose. She's clapping, beaming at her sister, but again and again, her eyes keep drifting back to mine, especially when she catches the bouquet.

Of course, she would catch the bouquet, and of course I force my eyes away when she does, but the same thing continues between us all the way through dinner. The speeches make everyone cry, including Rose from her seat at the head table. The pull toward her is magnetic, almost visceral. It doesn't help that I'm seated between two colleagues and positioned directly in her line of sight. I try to focus on my meal, on the conversations around me and the three-piece band when they start to play, but my attention keeps drifting back to Rose. The way she laughs at something Lily says, the graceful movement of her hand as she reaches for her glass—it's all so captivating that I keep missing people's words, even when several attractive women talk to me and try to tell me how great my piano pieces were.

After the plates are cleared and the band encourages everyone onto the dance floor, I watch as Rose excuses herself from the head table. At first, I think she's going to the ladies' room, but she pauses and turns around, then starts walking straight toward me. My heart rate picks up as she approaches and stops before me, a new determination set on her face.

"Doctor Bennett," she says, "care to dance?"

I can't help smiling as I stand, smoothing my jacket. "I thought you'd never ask, Doctor Carter."

She bites back a smile of her own, but even as we step onto the dance floor, surrounded by people we know, the tension between us makes it feel like we're plugged into electrical sockets. Her perfume fills my senses as she steps closer to me. We move together as the music swells around us and our bodies find a natural, effortless rhythm like they did in my apartment that night, skin on skin. I need to move on from this. But she's stuck in my head like a record, even when she's not right in front of me.

"You look beautiful," I tell her into her ear. The words tumble out before I can stop them. "I haven't been able to take my eyes off you all night, you know that?"

A blush creeps up her neck, but her gaze remains steady. "Is that so?"

"You know it is," I hear myself growl. "Rose, I—"

She cuts me off, her fingers tightening on my shoulder. "Lucas, let's not complicate things. We work together. People here can see us. It's—"

"I'm not your ex," I remind her again. I want to do bad things to her in this dress, tell her all the things I've been keeping in, in the only way I know how. By using my hands, my fingers, my entire body. She sighs, long and hard.

"I know you're not my ex. I'm so sorry I compared you to him. You're the opposite of him. You're..."

"I'm what?"

I pull her slightly closer, emboldened by the music, the atmosphere, the way she just fits right against me. "I'm yours. I want you. And I think you feel the same. You wouldn't have asked me to dance if you didn't. You wouldn't have agreed to let me play. I feel you watching me, Rose."

Rose looks up at me. "And I feel *you*. All the time. Everywhere."

The torture is clear in her emerald eyes and for a moment, I think she's going to pull away. Instead, she leans in and moans softly, right before her hand sweeps up to the back of my neck. Her lips press to mine in a kiss I know she didn't plan on, any more than I did. It's soft, lingering, filled with the aching I've been feeling, too. My hand cups her face; the other finds her waist but just as quickly, she pulls back. The aching transfers to her voice when she whispers at me, directly into my ear.

"It's a three-minute walk to my hotel room. Do you want to get out of here?"

* * *

The sex is just as incredible, if not more incredible than before. We move together like our bodies already know each other inside out. But I tell myself not to read into it, to just enjoy Lucas Bennett as we fall backward onto the hotel bed. He strips off my clothes with a fervor that sends shock waves of lust right down my spine and through every single inch of me.

I've been feeling his eyes on me all day and it's been turning me on so much, I couldn't deny myself another taste of him, whatever the consequences might be. I am done pushing him away. If he's happy with a casual thing, until I become a mother and start my new life, the life I've always dreamed of, then I'll be just fine with that.

His hands are rough and determined as they throw my shoes to the floor with my dress, but gentle as they trace delicate lines across my body. I could burst into flames of desire under this man. I can feel myself getting lost in his touch, forgetting everything else except the pure lightning-bolt pleasure through my veins as we become entwined on the hotel bed. I hear myself let out a deep, throaty moan that echoes off the cobalt blue walls.

"Oh, God," I mutter. "This is insane, Lucas."

His fingers trace circles around my palm as he continues kissing my neck, sucking and licking, picking up where we left off all those weeks ago, only he's a beast unleashed right now, someone who's clearly decided he wants me and wants to show me exactly how much. I'd be pretty terrified of what this all means if I wasn't so completely enraptured. "This is what you do to me, Doctor Carter."

I can feel his erection pressing against my stomach now, and I can't help but grind against him in anticipation. Why have I been denying myself…this? He pulls away from my neck, sucking on my earlobe as he whispers, "Do you want this? Do you want more of me?"

His voice is rough with lust and I nod and reach for him in turn, unable to form any words as he starts trailing kisses down my chest and teasingly nipping at my nipples. It feels like I'm being branded by fire, but I want more. I've never let a man this close to me emotionally, as well as physically, and I arch into him as he lowers his head between my legs. He takes a deep breath through his nose, inhaling me deeply, letting his fingers tease at me.

"So beautiful, every part of you, Rose." His breath fans across my skin, sending chills down my back. "I could never get enough of you." His lips on me make my toes curl as he begins to lick and suckle, and I gasp and writhe underneath his swirling tongue. He is driving me wild, tracing figure eights, and I grasp for him, pulling him closer to me with my legs, rocking my hips against his mouth. The friction only heightens the sensation coursing through my body. All I can think is how much more of this incredible feeling it's possible for me to handle without exploding.

He must be thinking the same, because he groans and repositions against me and thrusts. I shudder at the feeling of being one again. I love how our tongues dance hungrily as we move in sync, finding that rhythm we always find together, faster this time, harder, more animalistic. Maybe it's the thrill of the hotel room, the noise of the wedding downstairs, knowing we've been dancing circles around each other all this time, but it's so raw and intimate, and when we finally slow, it's like our bodies might have known each other before, in a different life or a different time, maybe. I fall into the magic of it all, taking over, climbing on top of him before we both finish this too soon.

My nails dig into Lucas's shoulders, leaving small red marks as I urge him closer. Slapping skin, rustling bedsheets, steamed-up windows. It's the most erotic encounter of my life so far. We make love two, three, maybe four more times. I lose count. It all blurs into one breathless tangle and we can't get enough of each other, but eventually, we can't hide out for much longer. People must be looking for the maid of honor by now.

The taste of him lingers on my lips as we walk back to the wedding party. My heart is still a speeding train. I'm torn between the urge to reach for his hand and the need to maintain a respectable distance. I sneak a glance at him as he goes for a well-earned drink, admiring how his suit hugs his broad shoulders, and how he's covertly hidden the wrinkles in his shirt quite expertly under his jacket and tie. I hope my face isn't too flushed. My lipstick was so smudged I just had to do my whole makeup again.

He catches my eye and smiles, and I feel high from our dirty little secret. We avoid each other for the best part of an hour, before he corners me in a quiet hallway away from the crowds.

"I've missed you," he groans, urging me close, pressing his lips to mine.

"That was…" I start, unsure how to finish the sentence. I'm too busy kissing him, melting right back into him.

"Incredible," Lucas offers, his deep voice tinged with amusement.

"Amazing," I agree, grinning under his mouth.

"There you two are!" Lily's voice cuts through the moment. My sister appears in a whirl of white lace, her face flushed with happiness and champagne. "Where have you been hiding?"

I open my mouth, but no words come out. Lucas smoothly steps in. "Just catching up. It's been a while."

Lily's eyes dart between us, a knowing smile playing on her lips. "Well, don't let me interrupt you *catching up*, whatever that means, wink-wink. But save a dance for me, Rose. We need photos of the flower girls on the dance floor!"

As she swirls away, I let out a breath. Lucas chuckles.

"Shall we?" he asks, gesturing back toward the party.

Throughout the evening, we gravitate toward each other like magnets. A brush of hands as we reach for champagne. Stolen kisses in quiet corners that leave me breathless and wanting more. But despite my happiness, something keeps niggling at me. If I am pregnant, this will all end. I cannot have one good thing without losing the other. I tell myself over and over not to let it bother me. I know I've been trying to psyche myself up for success after so much disappointment, but still, the chances of it actually working are slim, right?

CHAPTER NINETEEN

Three weeks later

THE DOORBELL CHIMES and I pull open the door, instantly overcome with the strange anticipation that always hits me when I see Rose. She looks nervous, her hands wrapped around the strap of her purse. I guess it's been a while since we've seen each other, since she took some time off to look after the twins, and I went to Atlanta for a conference, and to see Mom.

"My flower girl," I say with a grin, stepping aside to let her in. She smiles a little wider, but there's something off in her expression. I can't quite place it. "Come on in," I add, shutting the door behind her. The smell of garlic and herbs fills the apartment and I tell her I'm making something simple, comforting. I hope she'll like it.

"It smells amazing," she says, and I lean in, dropping a kiss on her cheek as I take her coat. She looks at me, her expression unreadable, but she doesn't lean in to kiss me back. Okay. Noted.

We walk to the kitchen together, where I've got pots of sauce simmering on the stove. I feel strangely proud, though I wouldn't normally admit that. "I'm trying out a new recipe from my mom," I tell her, giving the sauce a stir. "How've you been?"

"Busy," she says, her voice a bit strained. She starts twisting a piece of her hair around her finger. "The twins are a handful, but Lily and Theo had an amazing time in Barbados."

I nod, tossing in a bit more seasoning, watching her out of the corner of my eye. She seems jittery. Something's definitely off. "And how are the newlyweds?" I ask.

She forces a smile. "Blissfully happy. They're moving in to the new house soon."

She shifts her weight, glancing around the kitchen like she's not sure what to do with herself. "How was your business trip?" she asks.

"Productive, but long," I say, glancing at her. "Met a few guys doing some amazing new research—could be a game changer..." I trail off when I see her expression. It's way too tense for such casual conversation.

I hand her a bowl of cherry tomatoes, figuring maybe the simple task will get her to relax. "You can halve these for the salad."

We work side by side in silence, though I can feel her anxiety radiating off her. Every so often,

I brush her arm when I reach for something and I try to catch her eye, but she avoids my gaze. I can't take it anymore.

"So," I say after a moment, pausing with the spoon, "are you gonna tell me what's really on your mind?"

She sets down the knife and takes a deep breath. "Lucas, I..." Her voice falters, and I watch her struggle with whatever she's trying to say. Her fingers are trembling slightly. Then, all at once, she blurts it out. "I'm pregnant."

The words hit me like a punch. I freeze. The spoon slips from my hand and clatters onto the stove, splattering sauce everywhere. I don't care. I'm staring at her, my mind reeling, trying to process what she's just said.

"I did a home test first," she says quickly, her words spilling out in a rush. "Then I went to the fertility center for confirmation. It's positive."

I turn to the sink, gripping the edge, trying to steady myself. I take a deep breath, but it doesn't calm the tension coiling in my stomach. After a long pause, I manage to speak. "I should have expected this," I say. "The trial was a success, that's amazing." I shake my head. A mix of emotions that I can't even begin to sort out are roiling through me. "I'm happy for you, but..."

"What if it's yours?"

I whip around to face her as her question hits

me like another punch. "Wait. You think it could be *mine*?"

She goes pale, like she's about to crumble right in front of me. "I'm not sure," she whispers, avoiding my gaze. "I'd just had the procedure before the wedding...and we were together, several times. I mean, it's possible, right?"

Possible. I search my memory, but it's all a blur—a series of red-hot moments where I lost myself and everything else faded away. Did we use protection every time? I can't even remember, and that realization makes me feel sick.

"Jesus, Rose...what the hell?"

"I'm sorry," she whispers, looking like she's about to cry. And maybe I should feel more sympathy but right now I'm furious at myself. I know we've both made mistakes here, but this...this changes everything.

"What will happen if it's yours?" she asks.

I can hear the panic in the undertone and I start pacing.

"Rose, I never intended to be a father," I say, trying to keep my voice calm, despite the fear that's rising up from my core the harder I try to push it down. "It's not what I wanted. It's not what I planned for. I told you I didn't want—"

"I know. I know, but you said you wanted *me*. Doesn't that mean anything?"

I let out a laugh. I can't help it, it's the shock.

The absurdity of the whole thing, the irony. Her face falls, and I feel a pang of guilt, but I push it down and keep pacing. I'd be a terrible father; I'd regret it. I wouldn't ever be around, I'm too busy! She starts glancing toward the door.

"We'll have to do a test, together...you know that as well as I do. Oh, God, this is such a mess."

She grabs her purse, her movements jerky and tense. She's on the verge of breaking down, and I want to reach out, tell her it's going to be okay...but I don't even know if that's true. I drag a hand down my face, trying to sort through the utter turmoil taking over my chest. If it's mine, I can't... I mean, I can't be a father. I'd only mess it up, or regret it. I went over all this with Mabinty.

"I'm sorry," she whispers, her voice cracking. "I totally respect your decision to not want anything to do with me. I said I would do this alone and I will, whether it's yours or not."

"Rose, wait—" I start, but she's already halfway out the door.

"I'll let you know when the test is scheduled," she says over her shoulder. Her voice is flat and controlled, though I can see the tears in her eyes. And then she's gone, leaving me standing in the middle of my kitchen, the sauce still bubbling on the stove. I feel like the ground has just shifted under me, and I don't know how to get my footing back.

***

I slip through a gap in the chain-link fence, my boots crunching on broken glass and other bits of trash from years ago. The crumbling facade of the abandoned Chicago post office is a hulking relic of Art-Deco grandeur, now being left to decay. This is the first urban exploring adventure I've taken alone, without Lucas, but it doesn't intimidate me. I've got scarier things going on right now.

I think back to the test we took three days ago, to see if it was his. He didn't have to do much, just swab his cheek and hand it to me, but the whole exchange felt weird and dirty and he barely met my eyes as he handed the sample over. I felt as crushed as a dead beetle and I've been crushed ever since, having to work around him, feeling his eyes on me, the pitying looks. Like he wants to talk to me but knows there's nothing to say.

He did try to call me last night. He wanted to find out the results. I didn't have them then, so I sent him a message by way of answering his call.

No news yet.

I watched my phone all night for a message back, but it didn't come, and then the anger really sank in. At him, and myself, for getting into this stupid situation. For trusting him! He promised he wasn't like David and stupidly, I started to let my guard down. I even hoped for one tiny split second that maybe I wasn't pregnant, so I could be exactly what he wanted. As if that wouldn't have been doing myself the hugest, most unforgivable disservice! I promised never to bend for another man. Why should I?

Inside, I flick on my flashlight, illuminating a huge, cavernous sorting room and rows of very cool-looking rusted mail chutes. Dust motes swirl in the beam as I pick my way carefully across the plaster-strewn floor. What a mess. This place is only marginally messier than my life.

My mind drifts back to Lucas as I explore. The way he looked, standing in that kitchen three days ago, his sauce dripping all over the place. He was so repulsed by the possibility this child could be his, and now... I don't know how to tell him.

My phone beeps. Lily.

Have you had the results yet?

She knew I was getting them today, but I escaped with the news and came out here. I can't escape forever, though. And I owe it to Lucas to tell him first.

My flashlight beam catches on an old sorting table. I lean against it, lost in my thoughts. The cold metal seeps through my jacket and I click a few photos on my phone, absent-mindedly, lingering on one of us at the wedding. We look good together, I think. But I'm not what he wants; he already made that very clear.

"He has every right to not want a family, just as I have every right to want one," I say aloud as if any ghosts or birds that might be lingering here might hear me and agree. "But I know he'd be good at it. He'd be a great dad. He's just convinced himself he wouldn't be, because of his own father."

I sigh to myself. I am going to suffer the same fate with Lucas Bennett as Mabinty did.

I push off from the table and continue my aimless wandering. My footsteps echo off the high ceilings as my brain churns through the situation and what to do; how it blew my mind, having to do that paternity test the other day, and seeing the results this morning, staring up at me in black-and-white.

I stumble over a fallen beam, catching myself against a wall. The momentary shock clears my head, and Lucas's face is all I can see—his incredible smile, the light in his eyes when he talks about his work and his adventures, and his food. The way he looked up on stage that time, doing his thing alongside me. The way he looked at me when he told me I should just trust him.

"God, I've been an idiot," I groan, rubbing my face. "I never should have trusted him." The tears sting my eyes. "But I couldn't help it. I'm in love with him."

I sink to my knees on the filthy floor and sob, pouring out my distress into the silence. On reflection, abandoned buildings are great places to fall apart because no one can hear or see you, but I am pathetic, and I am pregnant and I have no idea how to tell him. "Ridiculous. My whole life is just ridiculous!"

After what feels like an eternity, I finally pull myself together. I just have to do it, I decide. I just have to tell him. Right now.

My heart shifts in place as he answers my call. I can literally feel it thudding erratically under my sweater. "Rose?"

"Lucas." I can tell he is nervous. "I have the results from our test."

"Don't tell me," he says quickly. "I don't want to hear it right now."

I suck in a breath as my heart breaks all over again. Then I sigh so loudly that a pigeon startles in a cracked window frame. "If that's how you really feel…"

"No, I mean I want to see you. I want to hear this from you in person," he says. "Where are you?"

"I'm…" I look around me at the mess. This is no place to meet Lucas. Besides, I don't want to ruin these adventures for myself in the future by connecting them with bad memories, and I am rather enjoying these urban explorations. I will enjoy them without him.

"Meet me back at the Botanic Garden," I tell him. I figure whatever happens, we will both need air.

CHAPTER TWENTY

THE SCENT OF jasmine hangs in the air, as heavy as my thoughts as I pace along the winding path to the spot where she said she would be. Lily's wedding in this very garden was so beautiful. It feels like forever ago already, and my mind keeps replaying those stolen moments with Rose. If I could go back in time, knowing what I know, would I still have done it? Would I still have made love to her?

My heart feels like it's about to burst out of my chest and I'm digging my nails so hard into my palms that it hurts. I know I've hurt her, but I've been doing some soul searching these past few days, and whatever the results are, I know it's Rose I want. I'm in love with her. I have to tell her that and let the cards fall where they may, I guess. It's just that every time I try to imagine myself as a dad, my own father's face swims into view. I hear him telling Mom I was too expensive. I see him closing that damn study door on me.

I shake my head to clear the image. "You're not

him," I remind myself firmly, and not for the first time since she told me this child might be mine. "And you're not Rose's ex, either. You are better than that. You are better for her."

Suddenly, I see her, standing in big winter boots and her red coat. A vision. The sound of my footsteps makes her turn around.

"You got here fast."

I smirk. "I probably got a few speeding tickets." I reach out to sweep a stray lock of hair behind her ear and I take a deep breath, steeling myself. She takes my hands. Is it fear I see flicker across her face? My heart is thudding. How is it possible that I'm actually standing here hoping to God the child inside her isn't someone else's? Hoping it's mine.

She has to force herself to meet my eyes. "Lucas, the baby…by some miracle, it's yours. Not the donor's."

I stare at her, feeling my eyes widen in shock. My grip on her hands tightens, and I can feel a slight tremor in her fingers. She looks away, probably expecting me to lose my cool once and for all, worse than I did in my kitchen, for which I am not proud at all. But I find I am laughing, with relief more than anything. "So…so it's really mine?"

She frowns in surprise and nods, the words falling out of her quickly now. "I know this is a lot to take in. You're probably in shock. I want you to know that I don't expect anything from you. I can handle this on my own. You don't need to be involved if you don't want to be."

As the words leave her mouth, my heart constricts. Deep down, I know that's not what she truly wants. I can see it on her face. "Rose…" I swipe a hand behind her head, and she gasps softly, stepping closer as I urge her to me. "I know you like to think you're strong and independent and more than capable, but I am going to be by your side through this, okay?"

She blinks at me. "But you said…"

"I'm so sorry. I said a lot of stupid stuff in a moment of shock."

I guide her to a bench and sit beside her, my voice low. "I never thought I'd be here, telling you all this, with you, pregnant! But I was an idiot. I was so caught up in my head, I shouldn't have reacted like I did, or left it this long without telling you I love you."

"Oh, Lucas." She presses a hand over her mouth at my words, and her eyes fill with tears as I take her other hand.

"Can you ever trust me again? I never wanted to hurt you, Rose. You're the best thing in Chicago besides the pizza. I was just unprepared!"

I pause, looking down. "I've got some hang-ups from my childhood, from my dad, as if you haven't realized that. I spent my whole life thinking I'd end up like him—working too hard, always too distracted. So, I've been convincing myself I shouldn't bring a kid into the world."

She reaches out to me. "I know, but Lucas, you're so much more than your job. And I've seen you with kids—the twins adore you. You're amazing with them."

"I want to believe that. I really do," I tell her. "And you should know it was never like this with Mabinty. We'd grown so far apart. But you…" I pause, my thumb caressing her cheek. "Meeting you has changed everything. You've shown me something else, flower girl. I knew you were different the second that smoothie came between us."

Rose sniffs and I press my lips to hers. She kisses me back, then cradles my face. "What are you saying here, Lucas?"

I kiss her again. "I'm saying I want to make this work. Us, the baby, all of it. I'll even find a new position at another hospital so we don't have to work together. I don't want to complicate things for you professionally."

She stares at me open-mouthed, like she's stunned by my offer. "No, Lucas. You don't need to do that. I'd be proud to work alongside you. I told you before you're nothing like David. Maybe I convinced myself you were a few times, to protect myself, or to stop myself falling for you, but it didn't work. I'm in love with you."

I lean in, resting my forehead against hers.

"This is wild," I murmur. Then I feel my mouth stretching out into a grin. "When I set you up with that trial, I knew I was helping you, but this…"

"You took that helpfulness to a whole new level." She laughs now, which makes me laugh, and for the first time in a long time I have the feeling that everything really will be okay. I'm not going to be afraid of being a father. In fact, it's growing on me the more I think about it. I would do anything with and for this amazing woman.

She presses her mouth to mine, and I wrap my arms around her, savoring the feel of her, drawing her strength and courage around me and making it my own. The gentle breeze carries the scent of a thousand flowers, and I can't help picturing the new life growing inside her. Our life.

"I know we have a lot to figure out," she says, opening her eyes to meet my gaze.

"We'll do it together," I tell her. "I promise you, Rose, I'll be here. For you, for our child. Or children? It could be twins, right?"

"It could be," she replies, and for a second she looks quite bewildered. It makes me laugh. If it's twins, even better. Even more to love.

I lean in, closing the distance between us again, and we kiss like we never stopped, like our mouths know how to fuse together as well as our minds and bodies do. Is this what it feels like to have it all?

She cups my face in her hands again. "I love

you, Lucas Bennett," she whispers, her voice thick with emotion.

Tears prick at my eyes and I'm so choked I can barely whisper back, "I love you, too, Rose Carter."

I pull her into me again, and in this moment, with the breeze tickling my skin and my arms around Rose, I feel a sense of peace I've never known before. Whatever the future holds, I know I've found the woman I will love for the rest of my life.

The air is crisp as we make our way through the quiet back streets of the empty neighborhood. The early-morning light casts an ethereal soft glow on the worn buildings around us as we trudge ahead with flasks of coffee. It's almost surreal to be out here, bundled up in jackets and scarves, with Lucas beside me and our baby girl, Eliza, nestled quietly in a sling against my chest. She's just a few months old, all soft cheeks and bright eyes that take in everything around her, and I'm not sure she knows yet how lucky she is to have her very first adventure with both her parents right here.

Lucas is grinning like a kid as he points out the route he mapped for us last night. We're exploring a half-abandoned gin distillery and Eliza's twin sister, Francesca, is gurgling away from her carrier on his back. Our fraternal twins are our world these days. Just adorable. Their smiles have everyone wrapped around their little fingers.

Lucas's excitement is infectious, and a flutter of a thrill grips my stomach as we approach the tall entrance, covered in graffiti. I can't believe he manages to find so many of these places, and they're always exciting. Or maybe I'm just excited to be seeing them with him... To think my life used to be all work, work, work and now it's so much more. We're always finding new ways to play and explore, even more so with Eliza and Francesca in the picture.

This particular place has been around since the Prohibition era, he tells me, but it's been years since anyone used it for anything but the occasional art installation.

"This way," he whispers, and we squeeze through a side gate. The rusty creak makes Eliza stir against me. She lets out a tiny contented sigh before settling straight back to sleep. I don't know how she does it. Lucas glances over. His eyes crinkle up in wonder and love before turning his head to blow a kiss at Francesca. Then he meets my gaze with a look that makes my own heart ache with absolute happiness. How did I get this lucky?

It's strange and wonderful at the same time to see this side of him—the once guarded man who didn't think he wanted children at all, who now practically melts at the sight of his own daughters! The girls can do no wrong in his eyes. He barely takes his eyes off them.

Inside the old building, the sunlight filters onto my back through the stained-glass windows as we walk. It's so cool in here, not eerie at all. Steel shafts and pipes glint in the beams of light, giving the place an even more mysterious, almost magical, feel. The air feels layered in here somehow, dense with the faintest traces of juniper and spice, as if the ghost of gin is still lingering in the rafters and clinging to the walls. I watch Lucas trail a hand along a line of old barrels stacked against one wall, breathing in the sour edge of long-evaporated alcohol. He was wary of me joining him on these outings while I was pregnant, and now, despite me promising to tread carefully, he is guarding my every move, stepping out in front of me and motioning me forward when the path is danger-free. I love this man!

Lucas pulls me gently toward a central chamber. "Check this out," he whispers, guiding us toward what must have once been the main brewing room. The space is huge, with towering copper vats and intricate pipes that wind along the ceiling like veins. Nature has reclaimed parts of it. Vines have crept through cracks in the walls, and a small tree is sprouting defiantly near the entrance.

"Imagine what it used to look like," I whisper.

"Oh, I am." Lucas's gaze shifts from the room

to me, then down to Eliza, still sleeping peacefully. "This might be my favorite adventure yet," he says, and I melt.

His attention shifts to something across the room and he gestures for me to follow. We step carefully until we reach an arched window frame; the glass is long gone now. It opens out to a view of the city skyline, bathed in gorgeous golden morning light. "It's breathtaking," I say. "I can see why you wanted us to come here at such an ungodly hour."

Lucas smiles that half smile that always makes my heart skip, before gently taking Eliza from my arms, cradling her close. One girl on his back, one close to his chest.

"Rose," he says, his face turning serious. "I have something I need to ask you."

I frown. "What is it?"

He reaches out and tucks a strand of hair behind my ear, his thumb grazing my cheek. And then, in one graceful motion, he lowers himself to one knee, still holding Eliza in his arms.

I clasp a hand to my mouth, my heart racing as it all sinks in. Oh. *Oh.*

"My beautiful girlfriend," he begins, and my heart leaps up to my mouth. "You've changed everything for me. I thought I knew what I wanted, what I didn't want, and then you came along and… Well, I threw a drink on you, and you went on to prove to me that the best plans in life are the ones you don't even make yourself. I'm so lucky to have met you."

I laugh through my tears and he reaches over Eliza to squeeze my hand.

"You've given me more than I ever thought I deserved—a family, a home, and a love that feels like something out of a dream, truly. I can't imagine my life without you now, and I don't want to." He takes a deep breath, looking up at me. "Rose—will you marry me?"

I'm crying now, full-on sobbing as I nod. I can't even find the words. "Yes," I finally manage. "Yes, Lucas, yes."

He rises and passes Eliza back to me, and as the sunlight streams onto us all through the open window, he leans down to kiss me. I feel like my heart might explode out of my chest—I can't wait to tell Lily.

When he pulls back, he presses his forehead to mine, and suddenly, we're both laughing and crying like lovestruck idiots. He slides the most beautiful ring onto my finger and instantly it catches the light, almost blinding me. This is totally crazy. It's so like him to propose to me here. But with Lucas by my side and our girls the picture of happiness and contentment on their first ever urban exploration, I know this is only the beginning of our adventure.

* * * * *

*If you missed the previous story in the
Twin Baby Bumps duet,
then check out*
A Daddy for Her Babies

*And if you enjoyed this story,
check out these other great reads from
Becky Wicks*

Nurse's Keralan Temptation
Tempted by the Outback Vet
Daring to Fall for the Single Dad

All available now!

Enjoyed your book?

Try the perfect subscription for Romance readers and get more great books like this delivered right to your door.

See why over 10+ million readers have tried Harlequin Reader Service.

Start with a Free Welcome Collection with free books and a gift—valued over $20.

Choose any series in print or ebook.
See website for details and order today:

TryReaderService.com/subscriptions